ARTHUR MILLER

The Crucible

with commentary and notes by
SUSAN C.W. ABBOTSON

Series Editor: Enoch Brater

D0543648

Bloomsbury Methuen Drama
An imprint of Bloomsbury Publishing Plc

B L O O M S B U R Y
LONDON · OXFORD · NEW YORK · NEW DELHI · SYDNEY

Bloomsbury Methuen Drama
An imprint of Bloomsbury Publishing Plc

Imprint previously known as Methuen Drama

50 Bedford Square	1385 Broadway
London	New York
WC1B 3DP	NY 10018
UK	USA

www.bloomsbury.com

**BLOOMSBURY, METHUEN DRAMA and
the Diana logo are trademarks of Bloomsbury Publishing Plc**

This edition first published 2010
Reprinted 2010, 2011, 2012, 2013 (three times), 2014, 2015

Chronology of Arthur Miller by Enoch Brater, with grateful thanks to the Arthur Miller
Society for permission to draw on their 'Brief Chronology of Arthur Miller's Life and Works'

Arthur Miller has asserted his right under the Copyright, Designs and
Patents Act, 1988, to be identified as author of this work.

British Library Cataloguing-in-Publication Data
A catalogue record for this book is available from the British Library.

ISBN: PB: 978–1-4081–0839-0
ePDF: 978–1-4742–2555-7
ePUB: 978–1-4742–2554-0

Library of Congress Cataloging-in-Publication Data
A catalog record for this book is available from the Library of Congress.

Series: Student Editions

Printed and bound in India

Contents

Arthur Miller: 1915–2005

1915   17 October: Arthur Asher Miller born in New York City,
       the second of Isidore (Izzy) and Augusta (Gussie) Barnett
       Miller's three children. His brother Kermit born in 1912,
       sister Joan 1922.

1920– Attends PS 24 in Harlem, then an upper-middle-
  28   class Jewish neighbourhood, where his mother went to
       the same school. The family lives in an apartment
       overlooking Central Park on the top floor of a six-storey
       building at 45 West 110th Street, between Lenox and Fifth
       Avenues. Takes piano lessons, goes to Hebrew school and
       ice-skates in the park. His Barnett grandparents are
       nearby on West 118th Street. In summers the extended
       family rents a bungalow in Far Rockaway. Sees his first
       play in 1923, a melodrama at the Schubert Theatre.

1928   His father's successful manufacturing business in the
       Garment District, the Miltex Coat and Suit Company,
       with as many as 800 workers, begins to see hard times
       faced with the looming Depression. The family moves
       from Manhattan to rural Brooklyn, where they live at
       1350 East 3rd Street, near Avenue M, in the same
       neighbourhood as his mother's two sisters, Annie
       Newman and Esther Balsam. Miller plants a pear tree in
       the backyard ('All I knew was cousins'). Celebrates his
       bar-mitzvah at the Avenue M Temple.

1930   Transfers from James Madison High School where he is
       reassigned to the newly built Abraham Lincoln High
       School on Ocean Parkway. Plays in the football team and
       injures his leg in a serious accident that will later excuse
       him from active military service. Academic record
       unimpressive, and he fails geometry twice.

1931   Early-morning delivery boy for a local bakery before
       going off to school; forced to stop when his bicycle is
       stolen. Works for his father during the summer vacation.

1933   Graduates from Abraham Lincoln High School and
       registers for night school at City College. He leaves after
       two weeks ('I just couldn't stay awake').

1933– Earns $15 a week as a clerk for Chadwick-

34   Delamater, an automobile-parts warehouse in a run-
down section of Manhattan that will later become the site
for the Lincoln Center for the Performing Arts. He is the
only Jewish employee, and experiences virulent anti-
Semitism for the first time.

1934   Writes to the Dean of the University of Michigan to
appeal against his second rejection and says he has
become a 'much more serious fellow' ('I still can't believe
they let me in'). Travels by bus to Ann Arbor for the
autumn semester, with plans to study journalism because
'Michigan was one of the few places that took writing
seriously'. Lives in a rooming house on South Division
Street and joins the *Michigan Daily* as reporter and night
editor; takes a non-speaking part in a student production
of Shakespeare's *King Henry VIII*. Moves to an attic room
at 411 North State Street and works part-time in an off-
campus laboratory feeding past-prime vegetables to
thousands of mice.

1936   Writes his first play, *No Villain*, in six days during semester
break and receives a Hopwood Award in Drama for $250
using the pseudonym 'Beyoum'. Changes his major to
English.

1937   Enrols in Professor Kenneth T. Rowe's playwriting class.
Rewrites *No Villain* as *They Too Arise* and receives a major
award of $1,250 from the Theatre Guild's Bureau of New
Plays (Thomas Lanier – later Tennessee – Williams was
another winner in the same competition). *They Too Arise* is
produced by the B'nai Brith Hillel Players in Detroit and
at the Lydia Mendelssohn Theatre in Ann Arbor.
Receives a second Hopwood Award for *Honors at Dawn*
when Susan Glaspell is one of the judges. Contributes to
The Gargoyle, the student humour magazine. Drives his
college friend Ralph Neaphus east to join the Abraham
Lincoln Brigade in the Spanish Civil War, but decides not
to go with him. Months later Neaphus, twenty-three, was
dead.

1938   Composes a prison play, *The Great Disobedience*, and revises
They Too Arise as *The Grass Still Grows*. Graduates from the
University of Michigan with a BA in English. Joins the
Federal Theater Project in New York to write radio plays
and scripts.

1939   The Federal Theater Project is shut down by conservative forces in Congress, and Miller goes on relief. Writes *Listen My Children* and *You're Next* with his friend and fellow Michigan alumnus, Norman Rosten. *William Ireland's Confession* is broadcast on the Columbia Workshop.

1940 Marries Mary Grace Slattery, his college sweetheart at the University of Michigan. They move into a small apartment at 62 Montague Street in Brooklyn Heights. Writes *The Golden Years*, a play about Montezuma, Cortez, and the European conquest and corruption of Mexico. *The Pussycat and the Plumber Who Was a Man* airs on CBS Radio. Makes a trip to North Carolina to collect dialect speech for the Folk Division of the Library of Congress.

1941– Works as a shipfitter's helper on the night shift at the
43 Brooklyn Navy Yard repairing battle-scarred war vessels from the North Atlantic fleet. Finishes additional radio plays, including *The Eagle's Nest* and *The Four Freedoms*. Completes *The Half-Bridge*. The one-act *That They May Win* is produced in New York.

1944 Daughter Jane is born. Prepares Ferenc Molnar's *The Guardsman* and Jane Austen's *Pride and Prejudice* for radio adaptation, and continues his own writing for the medium. Tours army camps in preparation for the draft of a screenplay called *The Story of G.I. Joe*, based on news reports written by the popular war correspondent Ernie Pyle (withdraws from the project when his role as author is compromised). Publishes *Situation Normal ...*, a book about this experience that highlights the real challenges returning soldiers encountered on re-entering civilian life. Dedicates the book to his brother, 'Lieutenant Kermit Miller, United States Infantry', a war hero. *The Man Who Had All the Luck* opens on Broadway but closes after six performances, including two previews. The play receives the Theater Guild National Award.

1945 Publishes *Focus*, a novel about anti-Semitism and moral blindness set in and around New York. His article 'Should Ezra Pound Be Shot?' appears in *New Masses*.

1946 Adapts *Three Men on a Horse* by George Abbott and John C. Holm for radio.

1947 *All My Sons* opens in New York and receives the New York Drama Critics' Circle Award; the Donaldson Award and the first Tony Award for best author. His son Robert is born. Moves with his family to a house he purchases at

31 Grace Court in Brooklyn Heights. Also buys a new car, a Studebaker, and a farmhouse in Roxbury, Connecticut. Writes the article 'Subsidized Theater' for the *New York Times*.

1948   Builds by himself a small studio on his Connecticut property where he writes *Death of a Salesman*. Edward G. Robinson and Burt Lancaster star in the film version of *All My Sons*.

1949   *Death of a Salesman*, starring Lee J. Cobb, Arthur Kennedy, Cameron Mitchell and Mildred Dunnock opens at the Morosco Theatre in New York on 10 February. Directed by Elia Kazan with designs by Jo Mielziner, it wins the New York Drama Critics' Circle Award, the Donaldson Prize, the Antoinette Perry Award, the Theatre Club Award and the Pulitzer Prize. His essay 'Tragedy and the Common Man' is printed in the *New York Times*. Attends the pro-Soviet Cultural and Scientific Conference for World Peace at the Waldorf-Astoria Hotel to chair a panel with Clifford Odets and Dimitri Shostakovich.

1950   Adaptation of Henrik Ibsen's *An Enemy of the People* produced on Broadway starring Fredric March and Florence Henderson ('I have made no secret of my early love for Ibsen's work'). First sound recording of *Death of a Salesman*. *The Hook*, a film script about graft and corruption in the closed world of longshoremen in the Red Hook section of Brooklyn, fails to reach production after backers yield to pressure from the House Committee on Un-American Activities. *On the Waterfront*, the Budd Schulberg–Elia Kazan collaboration featuring Marlon Brando, changes the setting to Hoboken, New Jersey, but is developed from the same concept, and is released four years later.

1951   Meets Marilyn Monroe. Fredric March in the role of Willy Loman for Columbia Pictures in the first film version of *Death of a Salesman*. Joseph Buloff translates the play into Yiddish; his production runs in New York and introduces Miller's play to Buenos Aires.

1952   Drives to Salem, Massachusetts, and visits the Historical Society, where he reads documents and researches the material he will use in *The Crucible*. Breaks with Kazan over the director's cooperation with HUAC.

1953   *The Crucible* wins the Donaldson Award and the Antoinette Perry Award when it opens in New York at the Martin Beck Theatre. Directs *All My Sons* for the Arden, Delaware.

1954   US State Department denies Miller a passport to attend the Belgian premiere of *The Crucible* in Brussels ('I wasn't embarrassed for myself; I was embarrassed for my country'). NBC broadcasts the first radio production of *Death of a Salesman*. Mingei Theater stages first Japanese translation of *Salesman* in Tokyo, where the play is received as a cautionary tale about the 'salaryman'.

1955   The one-act version of *A View from the Bridge* opens in New York on a double-bill with *A Memory of Two Mondays*. HUAC pressurises city officials to withdraw permission for Miller to make a film about juvenile delinquency set in New York.

1956   Lives in Nevada for six weeks in order to divorce Mary Slattery. Marries Marilyn Monroe. Subpoenaed to appear before HUAC on 21 June, he refuses to name names. Accepts an honorary degree as Doctor of Humane Letters from his alma mater, the University of Michigan. Jean-Paul Sartre writes screenplay for French adaptation of *The Crucible*, called *Les Sorcieres de Salem*; the film stars Yves Montand and Simone Signoret. Travels with Monroe to England, where he meets Laurence Olivier, her co-star in *The Prince and the Showgirl*. Peter Brook directs revised two-act version of *A View from the Bridge* in London at the New Watergate Theatre Club, as censors determined it could not be performed in public. 'Once Eddie had been squarely placed in his social context, among his people,' Miller noted, 'the myth-like feeling of the story emerged of itself ... Red Hook is full of Greek tragedies.'

1957   Cited for contempt of Congress for refusing to co-operate with HUAC. On the steps of the United States Congress, and with Monroe on his arm, he vows to appeal against the conviction. Monroe buys all members of Congress a year's subscription to *I.F. Stone's Weekly*. First television production of *Death of a Salesman* (ITA, UK). *Arthur Miller's Collected Plays* is published, and his short story, 'The Misfits', appears in *Esquire Magazine*.

1958–   The US Court of Appeals overturns his conviction
59   for contempt of Congress. Elected to the National Institute of Arts and Letters and receives the Gold Medal for Drama.

1961   Miller and Monroe divorce (granted in Mexico on the

grounds of 'incompatibility'). *The Misfits*, a black-and-white film directed by John Huston featuring the actress in her first serious dramatic role, is released for wide distribution. Miller calls his scenario 'an eastern western' and bases the plot on his short story of the same name. Co-stars include Clark Gable, Montgomery Clift, Eli Wallach and Thelma Ritter. *The Crucible: An Opera in Four Acts* by Robert Ward and Bernard Stambler is recorded. Sidney Lumet directs a movie version of *A View from the Bridge* with Raf Vallone and Carol Lawrence. Miller's mother, Augusta, dies.

1962   Marries Austrian-born Inge Morath, a photographer with Magnum, the agency founded in 1947 by Henri Cartier-Bresson. Marilyn Monroe, aged thirty-six, dies. His daughter, Rebecca Augusta, is born in September. NBC broadcasts an adaptation of *Focus* with James Whitmore and Colleen Dewhurst.

1963   Publishes a children's book, *Jane's Blanket*. Returns to Ann Arbor to deliver annual Hopwood Awards lecture, 'On Recognition'.

1964   Visits the Mauthausen death camp with Inge Morath and covers the Nazi trials in Frankfurt, Germany, for the *New York Herald Tribune*. Reconciles with Kazan. *Incident at Vichy*, whose through-line is 'It's not your guilt I want, it's your responsibility', opens in New York, as does *After the Fall*. The former is the first of the playwright's works to be banned in the Soviet Union. The latter Miller says 'is not about Marilyn' and that she is 'hardly the play's *raison d'etre*'.

1965   Elected president of PEN, the international organisation of writers dedicated to fighting all forms of censorship. American premiere of the two-act version of *A View from the Bridge* is performed Off-Broadway. Laurence Olivier's production of *The Crucible*, starring Colin Blakely and Joyce Redman, is staged in London at the Old Vic by the National Theatre. Returns to Ann Arbor, where his daughter Jane is now a student, to participate in the first teach-in in the US concerning the Vietnam conflict.

1966   First sound recording of *A View from the Bridge*. In Rome Marcello Mastroianni and Monica Vitti play the parts of Quentin and Maggie in Franco Zeffirelli's Italian production of *After the Fall*. Miller's father, Isidore, dies.

1967   *I Don't Need You Any More*, a collection of short stories, is

published. Sound recording of *Incident at Vichy*. Television
production of *The Crucible* is broadcast on CBS. Visits
Moscow and tries to persuade Soviet writers to join PEN.
Playwright-in-Residence at the University of Michigan.
His son, Daniel, is born in January.

1968   *The Price*, which the playwright called 'a quartet', 'the most
specific play I've ever written', opens on Broadway. Sound
recording of *After the Fall*. Attends the Democratic National
Convention in Chicago as a delegate from Roxbury,
Connecticut. Leads peace march against the war in South-
East Asia with the Reverend Sloan Coffin, Jr, at Yale
University in New Haven. *Death of a Salesman* sells its
millionth copy.

1969   *In Russia*, a collaborative project with text by Miller and
photography by Morath, is published. Visits Prague in a
show of support for Czech writers; meets Vaclav Havel.
Retires as president of PEN.

1970   Miller's works are banned in the Soviet Union, a result of
his efforts to free dissident writers. *Fame* and *The Reason
Why*, two one-act plays, are produced; the latter is filmed
at his home in Connecticut.

1971   Television productions of *A Memory of Two Mondays* on
PBS and *The Price* on NBC. Sound recording of *An Enemy
of the People*. *The Portable Arthur Miller* is published.

1972   *The Creation of the World and Other Business* opens at the
Schubert Theatre in New York on 30 November. Attends
the Democratic National Convention in Miami as a
delegate. First sound recording of *The Crucible*.

1973   PBS broadcasts Stacy Keach's television adaptation of
Incident at Vichy, with Harris Yulin as Leduc. Champions
the case of Peter Reilly, an eighteen-year-old falsely
convicted of manslaughter for his mother's murder; four
years later, all charges are dismissed. *After the Fall* with
Faye Dunaway is televised on NBC. Teaches mini-course
at the University of Michigan; students perform early
drafts of scenes from *The American Clock*.

1974   *Up from Paradise*, musical version of *The Creation of the World
and Other Business*, is staged at the Power Center for the
Performing Arts at the University of Michigan. With
music by Stanley Silverman and cover design by Al
Hirschfield, Miller calls it his 'heavenly cabaret'.

1977   A second collaborative project with Inge Morath, *In the*

Country, is published. Petitions the Czech government to halt arrests of dissident writers. The *Archbishop's Ceiling* opens at the Kennedy Center in Washington, DC. Miller said he wanted to dramatise 'what happens ... when people know they are ... at all times talking to Power, whether through a bug or a friend who really is an informer'.

1978   *The Theater Essays of Arthur Miller* is published. NBC broadcasts the film of *Fame* starring Richard Benjamin. Belgian National Theatre mounts the twenty-fifth anniversary production of *The Crucible*; this time Miller can attend.

1979   *Chinese Encounters*, with Inge Morath, is published. Michael Rudman directs a major revival of *Death of a Salesman* at the National Theatre in London, with Warren Mitchell as Willy Loman.

1980   *Playing for Time*, the film based on Fania Fenelon's autobiography *The Musicians of Auschwitz*, is broadcast nationally on CBS, with Vanessa Redgrave and Jane Alexander. ('I tried to treat it as a story meaningful to the survivors, by which I mean all of us. I didn't want it to be a mere horror story.') *The American Clock* has its first performance at the Spoleto Festival in South Carolina, then opens in New York with the playwright's sister, Joan Copeland, as Rose Baum, a role based on their mother. Miller sees his play as 'a mural', 'a mosaic', 'a story of America talking to itself ... There's never been a society that hasn't had a clock running on it, and you can't help wondering – How long?'

1981   Second volume of *Arthur Miller's Collected Plays* is published. Delivers keynote address on the fiftieth anniversary of the Hopwood Awards Program in Ann Arbor.

1982   Two one-act plays that represent 'the colors of memory', *Elegy for a Lady* and *Some Kind of Love Story*, are produced as a double-bill at the Long Wharf Theatre in Connecticut under the title *2 by A.M.*

1983   Directs *Death of a Salesman* at the People's Art Theatre in Beijing, part of a cultural exchange to mark the early stage of the opening of diplomatic relations between the United States and the People's Republic of China. Ying Ruocheng plays Willy Loman in his own Chinese

translation. *I Think About You a Great Deal*, a monologue
written as a tribute to Vaclav Havel, appears in *Cross
Currents*, University of Michigan.

1984   *'Salesman' in Beijing* is published. The texts of *Elegy for a
Lady* and *Some Kind of Love Story* are printed under a new
title, *Two-Way Mirror*. Receives Kennedy Center Honors
for lifetime achievement. Reworks the script of *The
American Clock* for Peter Wood's London production at the
National Theatre.

1985   Twenty-five million viewers see Dustin Hoffman play
Willy Loman, with John Malkovich as Biff and Kate Reid
as Linda in the production of *Death of a Salesman* shown on
CBS. Goes to Turkey with Harold Pinter for PEN as an
ambassador for freedom of speech. Serves as delegate at a
meeting of Soviet and American writers in Vilnius,
Lithuania, where he attacks Russian authorities for their
continuing anti-Semitism and persecution of *samizdat*
writers. *The Archbishop's Ceiling* is produced in the UK by
the Bristol Old Vic. Completes adaptation of *Playing for
Time* as a stage play.

1986   One of fifteen writers and scientists invited to meet
Mikhail Gorbachev to discuss Soviet policies. The Royal
Shakespeare Company uses a revised script of *The
Archbishop's Ceiling* for its London production in the
Barbican Pit.

1987   Miller publishes *Timebends: A Life*, his autobiography.
Characterising it as 'a preemptive strike' against future
chroniclers, he discusses his relationship with Marilyn
Monroe in public for the first time. *Clara* and *I Can't
Remember Anything* open as a double-bill at Lincoln Center
in New York under the title *Danger: Memory!* Broadcasts of
The Golden Years on BBC Radio and Jack O'Brien's
television production of *All My Sons* on PBS. Michael
Gambon stars as Eddie Carbone in Alan Ayckbourn's
intimate production of *A View from the Bridge* at the
National Theatre in London. University of East Anglia
names its site for American Studies the Arthur Miller
Centre.

1988   Publishes 'Waiting for the Teacher', a nineteen-stanza free-
verse poem, in *Ha'aretz*, the Tel Aviv-based liberal
newspaper, on the occasion of the fiftieth anniversary of the
founding of the State of Israel.

1990   *Everybody Wins*, directed by Karel Reisz with Debra
        Winger and Nick Nolte, is released: 'Through the evolution
        of the story – a murder that took place before the story
        opens – we will be put through an exercise in experiencing
        reality and unreality.' Television production of *An Enemy of
        the People* on PBS. Josette Simon plays Maggie as a sultry
        jazz singer in Michael Blakemore's London revival of *After
        the Fall* at the National Theatre, where *The Crucible* also
        joins the season's repertory in Howard Davies's production
        starring Zoë Wannamaker and Tom Wilkinson. Updated
        version of *The Man Who Had All the Luck* is staged by Paul
        Unwin in a joint production by the Bristol Old Vic and the
        Young Vic in London.

1991   *The Last Yankee* premieres as a one-act play. *The Ride Down
        Mount Morgan*, 'a moral farce', has its world premiere in
        London: 'The play is really a kind of nightmare.'
        Television adaptation of *Clara* on the Arts &
        Entertainment Network. Receives Mellon Bank Award
        for lifetime achievement in the humanities.

1992   *Homely Girl, A Life* is published with artwork by Louise
        Bourgeois in a Peter Blum edition. Writes satirical op-ed
        piece for the *New York Times* urging an end to capital
        punishment in the US.

1993   Expanded version of *The Last Yankee* opens at the
        Manhattan Theatre Club in New York. Television
        version of *The American Clock* on TNT with the
        playwright's daughter, Rebecca, in the role of Edie.

1994   *Broken Glass*, a work 'full of ambiguities' that takes 'us back
        to the time when the social contract was being torn up',
        has a pre-Broadway run at the Long Wharf Theatre in
        Connecticut; opens at the Booth Theatre in New York on
        24 April. David Thacker's London production wins the
        Olivier Award for Best Play.

1995   Tributes to the playwright on the occasion of his eightieth
        birthday are held in England and the US. Receives
        William Inge Festival Award for Distinguished
        Achievement in American Theater. *Homely Girl, A Life and
        Other Stories*, is published. In England the collection
        appears under the title *Plain Girl*. Darryl V. Jones directs a
        production of *A View from the Bridge* in Washington, DC,
        and resets the play in a community of Domincan
        immigrants. The Arthur Miller Society is founded by

Steve Centola.

1996   Revised and expanded edition of *The Theater Essays of
        Arthur Miller* is published. Receives the Edward Albee Last
        Frontier Playwright Award. Rebecca Miller and Daniel
        Day-Lewis are married.

1997   *The Crucible*, produced by the playwright's son, Robert A.
        Miller, is released for wide distribution and is nominated
        for an Academy Award. Revised version of *The Ride Down
        Mount Morgan* performed at the Williamstown Playhouse in
        Massachusetts. BBC airs television version of *Broken Glass*,
        with Margot Leicester and Henry Goodman repeating
        their roles from the award-winning London production.

1998   *Mr Peters' Connections* opens in New York with Peter Falk.
        Revival of *A View from the Bridge* by the Roundabout
        Theatre Company wins two Tony Awards. Revised
        version of *The Ride Down Mount Morgan* on Broadway.
        Miller is named Distinguished Inaugural Senior Fellow of
        the American Academy in Berlin.

1999   Robert Falls's fiftieth anniversary production of *Death of a
        Salesman*, featuring Brian Dennehy as Willy Loman, moves
        from the Goodman Theater in Chicago and opens on
        Broadway, where it wins the Tony Award for Best Revival
        of a Play. Co-authors the libretto with Arnold Weinstein
        for William Bolcom's opera of *A View from the Bridge*, which
        has its world premiere at the Lyric Opera of Chicago.

2000   Patrick Stewart reprises his role as Lyman Felt in *The Ride
        Down Mount Morgan* on Broadway, where *The Price* is also
        revived (with Harris Yulin). Major eighty-fifth birthday
        celebrations are organised by Christopher Bigsby at the
        University of East Anglia and by Enoch Brater at the
        University of Michigan, where plans are announced to
        build a new theatre named in his honour; it opens
        officially on 29 March 2007 ('whoever thought when I
        was saving $500 to come to the University of Michigan
        that it would come to this'). 'Up to a certain point the
        human being is completely unpredictable. That's what
        keeps me going … You live long enough, you don't rust.'
        Echoes Down the Corridor, a collection of essays from 1944 to
        2000, is published. Miller and Morath travel to Cuba
        with William and Rose Styron and meet Fidel Castro and
        the Colombian writer Gabriel García Márquez.

2001   Williamstown Theater Festival revives *The Man Who Had*

All the Luck. Laura Dern and William H. Macy star in a film based on the 1945 novel *Focus.* Miller is named the Jefferson Lecturer in the Humanities by NEH and receives the John H. Finley Award for Exemplary Service to New York City. His speech *On Politics and the Art of Acting* is published.

2002   Revivals in New York of *The Man Who Had All the Luck* and *The Crucible,* the latter with Liam Neeson as John Proctor. *Resurrection Blues* has its world premiere at the Guthrie Theatre in Minneapolis. Miller receives a major international award in Spain, the Premio Principe de Asturias de las Letras. Death of Inge Morath.

2003   Awarded the Jerusalem Prize. His brother, Kermit Miller, dies on 17 October. *The Price* is performed at the Tricycle Theatre in London.

2004   *Finishing the Picture* opens at the Goodman Theatre in Chicago. *After the Fall* revived in New York. Appears on a panel at the University of Michigan with Mark Lamos, who directs students in scenes from Miller's rarely performed plays.

2005   Miller dies of heart failure in his Connecticut home on 10 February. Public memorial service is held on 9 May at the Majestic Theatre in New York, with 1,500 in attendance. Asked what he wanted to be remembered for, the playwright said, 'A few good parts for actors.'

Plot

Act One

Set in the Puritan town of Salem, Massachusetts, in 1692, *The Crucible* begins in the sparsely furnished bedroom of Reverend Samuel Parris's daughter, Betty, who is in a coma. His West Indian slave, Tituba, asks after Betty but is sent away. Parris, who spied Betty and her friends in the woods the night before, worries about how his parishioners will react to rumours that witchcraft is afoot. He questions his niece, Abigail Williams, who insists they were only dancing. Abigail has been dismissed from the Proctors' service under suspicious circumstances, but she asserts her innocence, saying that Elizabeth Proctor is spreading lies about her. Ann and Thomas Putnam's daughter, Ruth, is also acting strangely and they arrive to raise additional suspicions. Insisting that witchcraft is at fault, they encourage Parris to lead the townspeople outside in prayer. He agrees as the Putnams are important in the community, and he wants to stay in their favour.

Meanwhile, we learn more about what happened in the woods from a discussion between Abigail and two other servant girls who arrive, Mercy Lewis and Mary Warren. Mercy was dancing naked and Abigail was involved in a spell to harm Elizabeth Proctor, while Mary had watched from behind the trees. When they forcefully wake Betty she tries to fly. She is threatened by Abigail not to reveal the truth. John Proctor arrives to find out what is going on and send his servant, Mary, home. Proctor is left alone with Abigail. She admits the girls were playing games in the woods but were not involved in witchcraft. She also complains of his neglect, and it is clear that she believes he still has feelings for her. He insists they will never be together again. Betty screams and the others return, along with two elders, Rebecca Nurse and Giles Corey. Rebecca calms Betty, while Proctor antagonises Parris by accusing him of stirring up unfounded suspicions. Proctor states his dislike of Parris's authority and Putnam gets drawn into an argument over property. Reverend Hale, who has been sent for by Parris, arrives to interrogate the people of Salem.

Hale, rather pompously, takes charge. Proctor leaves, unhappy with the idea of a witchhunt, warning Hale to be circumspect. Ann confesses she sent her daughter to Tituba to ask her to conjure up the dead to find out why Ann has lost seven children in childbirth. Rebecca dislikes this superstitious conversation and leaves. Giles asks Hale about his own wife's tendency to read books, explaining that it disturbs his praying. Hale and Parris question Betty, who does not respond. They question Abigail further about events in the woods. She blames Tituba, saying that Tituba made her drink blood and tempted her to ally herself with the Devil. Tituba denies she has any contact with the Devil, but when Parris declares, 'You will confess yourself or I will take you out and whip you to your death', she becomes fearful for her life. Tituba confesses and is led by her questioners to name Sarah Good and Goody Osburn as conspirators. Abigail and Betty add more names and the adults scurry to arrest the accused.

Act Two
Eight days later at the Proctors' house, we see evident tension between Elizabeth and Proctor as she is hurt over his affair with Abigail, and he feels guilty. He has tried to make amends and is annoyed by her lack of forgiveness, but she suspects that he still harbours feelings for the girl. Mary has become an official of a court organised to try the witches, and fourteen people are in jail. Elizabeth urges Proctor to proclaim what Abigail said about the girls only playing games. He is fearful that he will not be believed and grows angry at Elizabeth's continued suspicion. Mary returns and gives Elizabeth a poppet, a homemade doll, which she has sewn while sitting in court. She informs them of the escalation of arrests and threatened hangings, saying

that even Elizabeth has been suspect. She insists she spoke in Elizabeth's defence, but recognising her newly acquired power, stands up to Proctor when he threatens her, before going to bed. Realising his wife's danger, Proctor agrees to go to town. At this point, Hale arrives.

Hale is uncertain about the girls' latest accusations, but sure that evil is at work. He has just come from Rebecca Nurse, whose name has also been mentioned. He questions the couple about their religious adherence, asking why they do not regularly attend church, and why their youngest son is not baptised. Proctor admits he dislikes Parris, but has done many things for the church. When asked to name the Ten Commandments, he significantly forgets adultery, until his wife reminds him. At Elizabeth's prompting Proctor shares his doubts about Abigail's veracity, but Hale is unsure. Francis Nurse and Giles arrive to announce their wives have been arrested. Hale is shaken, but insists the court will be fair, a belief he reasserts as the Marshal arrives to arrest Elizabeth, who has been denounced by Abigail. They take the poppet as proof that Elizabeth has been involved in questionable practices. It has a needle in its stomach, and Abigail has behaved in court as if someone were stabbing her. Although Mary insists she made the poppet and gave it to Elizabeth, Elizabeth's violent response to Abigail's accusations, insisting that, 'She must be ripped out of the world', convinces them that she needs to be cross-examined. Although Proctor angrily tears the warrant, his wife agrees to go. The husbands urge Hale to act, but as he insists that the town must be guilty of something for this to have happened, Proctor falls silent, evidently thinking about his own sin. Left alone with Mary, Proctor insists she help him clear his wife, but she is fearful of Abigail. He asserts a preparedness to confess his own adultery to destroy the court's faith in Abigail.

Act Three

In an anteroom outside the courtroom, we overhear Judge Hathorne cross-examine Martha Corey. Giles disrupts the proceedings to defend her and is brought before the court by Governor Danforth, who is now in charge. Francis, whose wife, Rebecca, has been condemned, also comes forth to insist the girls are lying. Though threatened with contempt, he and Giles stand firm. Proctor arrives with Mary as their witness, for he has convinced her that she must testify against Abigail. Danforth fears that Proctor is trying to undermine his court, rather than just save his wife. Elizabeth has declared herself pregnant, and Proctor insists it must be true as his wife is incapable of lying. Pointing out they will not hang a pregnant woman, Danforth suggests Proctor drop his protest, but Proctor refuses, as other innocents are involved. Danforth is shown a list of people who feel the wives are wrongly accused, but to the horror of the husbands, he orders everyone on the list to be arrested for questioning. Giles accuses Putnam of prompting his daughter to cry witchery on people to get their property, but when he refuses to name his source, he is arrested. Hale is becoming concerned about these high-handed responses, his doubts evidently on the rise, and he suggests a lawyer be engaged to deal with Mary, but Danforth insists on continuing the investigation himself. Danforth harshly questions Mary, but with encouragement from Proctor she stands firm.

Danforth has Abigail and the girls brought in to defend themselves. Abigail tries to deflect the charges, but Proctor's insistence on her bad character begins to make Danforth unsure. Proctor gets Parris to confess to seeing Abigail dance in the woods to help build his case. To reassert control, Hathorne asks Mary to illustrate how she pretends to faint in court. When she cannot, they decide she must be lying. Abigail leads the girls to act as if Mary were sending a spirit against them, and Mary panics. Proctor pronounces Abigail to be a whore and confesses his adultery. Since Abigail denies it, Elizabeth is brought to confirm the charge, as Proctor says she knew. Not knowing her husband has confessed, she lies to save his reputation and declares no adultery took place. Despite Hale's claims that it was 'a natural lie to tell', Danforth refuses to believe adultery has taken place. As the girls reassert that Mary's spirit is attacking them, Mary breaks down and accuses Proctor of being in league with the Devil. All the judges, except Hale (who now denounces the proceedings), are convinced by this performance, and have Proctor arrested. When asked to confess, Proctor declares that 'God is dead', and accuses them of being damned for their part in such events.

Act Four

Three months have passed and Sarah Good and Tituba, who confessed themselves witches, languish in jail. A drunken Marshal Herrick moves them to a different cell as they call to the Devil for release. Danforth and Hathorne, having had twelve people hanged, are about to hang seven more, including Proctor, Rebecca and Martha. Hale is advising prisoners to confess to avoid death, and they feel that Parris is becoming unhinged by the pressure. They hope to get someone to confess to make their case valid, and Parris suggests delaying the executions. Abigail and Mercy have absconded with his savings, and he is fearful that the rumoured rebellion in nearby Andover will spread to Salem. Hale enters to admit his failure in getting Rebecca to confess and demands that those awaiting execution be pardoned. Danforth insists they must continue, to justify the case against those already hanged.

They decide to ask Elizabeth to encourage her husband to confess, and although she suspects a trick, she agrees to speak with Proctor. Left alone with her husband, we see by their physical descriptions that both have suffered in jail. Elizabeth relates how Giles died under torture and Proctor confides his decision to confess, not feeling worthy enough to die beside Rebecca and Martha. Elizabeth insists on his worthiness and shoulders blame over his adultery because of her former coldness. She leaves him to make his own decision, but wanting to live for her sake, he announces he will give them the confession they want.

The judges return, excited about Proctor's confession, to which they bring a horrified Rebecca as witness. To

Proctor's growing discomfort, they have Cheever write it down for Proctor to sign. However, Proctor refuses to name anyone else as an accomplice, and although he signs the confession, he refuses to hand it over for public display, knowing it will be used against the others. Admitting his confession is a lie, he tears it apart. Proctor recognises the dignity of his moral stance and chooses to die beside the others. Danforth orders the hangings to proceed, and Proctor and Rebecca are taken outside. First Parris, then Hale plead with Elizabeth to intervene, but honouring her husband's decision, she refuses. The curtain falls to the sound of the drums heralding the executions.

Appendix

Miller wrote a short additional scene for Act Two, not always included in performance, which takes place five weeks after Elizabeth has been arrested, on the day before her trial. Proctor secretly meets Abigail to warn her to tell the truth or be exposed, but Abigail does not believe him. She seems close to madness: still passionate about Proctor, and paranoid about the township. Her body is covered in scars she believes caused by spirits. She refuses to help and Proctor is left with few options.

Afterword

'Echoes Down the Corridor' is a brief note which follows the play, in which Miller relates subsequent events. Parris is voted from office, Abigail is alleged to have become a Boston prostitute, and Elizabeth eventually remarries. Twenty years on from these proceedings, the government awarded compensation to the victims still living, and to the families of the dead.

Commentary

Context – historical, social and theatrical

The Crucible takes for its point of departure the Salem witch trials of 1692, but it also reflects Miller's reaction to how the House Un-American Activities Committee (HUAC) operated at the time when the play was written, and the dangers of the McCarthyist fervour that gripped America in the 1950s. It is typical of his work in its sense of purpose, humanity and the desire to bring society to a better understanding of itself.

Salem witch trials

Miller's interest in the Salem witch trials was prompted by reading Marion Starkey's *The Devil in Massachusetts* (1949), which suggested that attitudes towards race and nationality during the Second World War made the Salem witch trials an allegory for that period. While Miller saw additional parallels in the climate of the 1950s, he decided to research the original trials by visiting the Historical Society in Salem, Massachusetts. Miller found the core of his plot in Charles W. Upham's 1867 *Salem Witchcraft*, in which all of the play's characters are referred to and many of its events related. He also read the original court transcripts.

Salem was settled in 1629, but by the 1690s had become divided between the agricultural farms of Salem Village and the adjacent, more mercantile port of Salem Town. There was much rivalry between the two, and jealousy of those like the Nurses and Proctors who owned property on the lucrative roadway between them. In January 1692, the Reverend Parris's daughter, Betty, aged nine, and her cousin, Abigail, aged eleven, apparently became afflicted with contortions and fits, making complaints about being pinched and pricked with pins. After the local doctor found no physical evidence for their condition, and other girls experienced the same symptoms, witchcraft was suspected. Parris's slave, Tituba, was asked to bake a 'witch cake' to discover who was responsible for this. Soon after, Thomas Putnam and other men of the town accused Tituba and two disreputable women of the neighbourhood, Sarah Good and Sarah Osborne, of causing the afflictions. Examined in March by the local magistrates John Hathorne and Jonathan Corwin, Tituba confessed, and all three were sent to jail in Boston. More accusations followed from the girls, including ones against Martha Corey, who had voiced scepticism over their credibility, as well as Rebecca Nurse and Elizabeth Proctor. The local innkeeper John Proctor, who had written to Boston complaining about the proceedings, was imprisoned in April after objecting to his wife's arrest during Deputy-Governor Danforth's examination. Even a former minister of the town, George Burroughs, was accused, and three of Proctor's children. After Osborne had died in jail, magistrates were assigned to trials beginning in May, by which month's end there were sixty-two people in custody and more to follow.

Most of the accused were found guilty on controversial and questionable evidence. The afflicted would claim an apparition of the accused had attacked them, and since the courts decided that the Devil needed a person's permission to take their bodily form, the accusations were considered believable. Some confessed, usually after being unpleasantly cross-examined, or condemning testimony was given against them from other self-confessed witches. Discoveries of poppets, ointments, horoscopes or books on palmistry were also considered as evidence against them. Though several men were accused, the majority were women, as they were considered the weaker gender and therefore more susceptible to the Devil. After being interrogated, the accused would later stand trial, at which most were condemned to death. The first to be hanged on 10 June was Bridget Bishop, an outspoken woman close to sixty years old; she claimed innocence to the moment of her death.

Rebecca Nurse, Sarah Good and three more women were hanged in July. Elizabeth was given a stay of execution because she was pregnant, but Proctor was hanged alongside Burroughs and three others on 19 August. Burroughs unsettled onlookers by reciting the Lord's Prayer on the scaffold, a feat supposedly impossible for an agent of the Devil. Martha was hanged in September along with seven others. All were excommunicated and none were allowed proper burial.

The courts were dismissed in October after several complaints, and when they reconvened the following year, with Danforth serving for the first time, evidence based on apparitions was no longer admissible. Although three additional women were found guilty, many charges were dismissed. There were no more hangings, and by March the trials had been much discredited. By May, Elizabeth and the rest of the prisoners were released. One judge, Samuel Sewall, repudiated the trials and formerly apologised; he would go on to write the first attack on slavery in America. Hale, who was the great-grandfather of the American Revolutionary War hero Nathan Hale, had changed his mind late in the court proceedings after his wife was accused of witchcraft. She was acquitted and he would go on to speak out against the trials, publishing a highly critical text of the proceedings in 1697, *A Modest Enquiry into the Nature of Witchcraft*. In 1702 the General Court declared the 1692 trials unlawful, and by 1711 restitutions were made to victims. In 1752 Salem Village was renamed Danvers, but it would not be until 1957 that Massachusetts made a formal apology for the debacle. In 1992, on the three-hundredth anniversary of the trials, a park in Salem was opened with a stone bench in memory of those executed; Miller spoke at the dedication ceremony.

In a note at the beginning of the play Miller declares that his account is predominantly truthful, and while he has made some changes for 'dramatic purposes', the nature of the events themselves is historically accurate. The major alterations are the fusing of various original characters into a single representative, reducing both the number of judges

and the girls 'crying out', slight alterations to the time-line
and locations, decreasing Proctor's age (originally in his
sixties, with Elizabeth, his third wife, twenty years his junior)
and increasing Abigail's age to allow the possibility of an
affair, as well as making her the girl who denounces
Elizabeth. While he based characters on what he learned
through letters, records and reports, Miller asks for them to
be properly considered as 'creations of my own, drawn to
the best of my ability in conformity with their known
behavior'. Despite this disclaimer, critics have noticed a
number of the play's historical inaccuracies. Since the 1958
edition, however, the play contains additional notes
detailing the situation of Salem society in the 1690s. These
supply facts regarding the lives of the main characters
involved that go beyond the events of the play itself, and
stand as a tribute to the extent of Miller's research.

Many details in the play are firmly supported by trial
transcripts and other records of the time, such as Sarah
Good's condemnation on being unable to recite the Ten
Commandments, the Putnams' rivalry and desire for more
land, Rebecca's steadfast claim of innocence, Giles Corey's
complaint against his wife preventing him from saying his
prayers and his death by being crushed under stones. There
is also proof of Mary Warren's poppet being given to
Elizabeth, Mary's repudiation of the girls' accusations and
subsequent change of heart. Notable details from Miller's
dramatic imagination include the presentation of Abigail
and her lust for Proctor; the character development of both
the Proctors, with John especially depicted as a liberated
thinker; and Proctor's subsequent confession, recantation,
and death alongside Rebecca and Martha (all three were
hanged on different dates). Miller also makes Governor
Danforth and Reverend Hale the central and direct
antagonists to Proctor. Hathorne (the great-great-
grandfather of the writer Nathaniel Hawthorne) was
probably the most despicable of the real judges, being the
only one who never publicly repented the key part he played
in the trials. It was the uncompromising moral absolutism of
that era's Puritans that Miller wished to capture and expose.

The original prosecution was as blind to facts and relentless as they appear to be in the play; and there were many, like the Putnams, who took full mercenary advantage of the situation or stood by and allowed the atrocities to happen.

House Committee on Un-American Activities (HUAC)
The concept of HUAC had begun in 1938 with the Dies Committee, charged with investigating German-American involvement in Nazi and Ku Klux Klan activity, but the committee soon became more interested in the communist threat. This committee had been behind the closing of the Federal Theater Project that Miller had briefly joined after his graduation from the University of Michigan. They concluded, erroneously, that it was being overly influenced by the Communist Party. HUAC became a permanent committee in 1946 charged to investigate suspected threats of subversion or propaganda that attacked 'the form of government guaranteed by our Constitution', but their real target was anyone who exhibited left-of-centre sympathies. People were subpoenaed to prove that they were not or had never been active in the Communist Party. If they confessed to any such activity, they were expected to name names of anyone else who might have been involved. It was not illegal to belong to the Communist Party, but HUAC could convict anyone of contempt if they refused to cooperate, and send them to jail. This conveyed an implication that to be a communist sympathiser was a criminal act, despite the laws of the United States. People were often called before HUAC on inconclusive or even questionable evidence; and even if the committee's investigation came up empty, many lives were subsequently ruined. Suspicion and ostracism led to loss of employment and the end of many professional careers.

Few noticed while the committee investigated government employees, but when it began to go after more prominent public figures in the entertainment industry, beginning with an investigation into alleged communist propaganda in the Hollywood film industry, HUAC caught people's attention. After nine days of hearings in 1947, a group of writers and actors was convicted on charges of contempt of Congress for refusal to answer questions. Each of 'The Hollywood Ten', as they became known, took the Fifth Amendment, refusing to testify on the grounds that they might incriminate themselves. Even though none had confessed to any communist sympathies, they were sent to jail for sentences ranging from six to twelve months and subsequently 'blacklisted', which meant they would not be offered work. The example of such harsh treatment scared many into going along with whatever the committee asked, rather than face punishment themselves. The hearings escalated in the 1950s and the anti-communist fervour they provoked became known as McCarthyism, named after its instigator, Senator Joseph McCarthy. His involvement began in 1950 with a speech to a Republican Women's Club. A flood of press attention followed when he produced a piece of paper that he claimed contained a list of known communists working for the State Department.

Although McCarthy would serve on committees covering both government and military investigations into communist infiltration, as a United States senator he did not serve on HUAC, although his scaremongering helped create the atmosphere that gave the House Committee its credibility. In Miller's 1999 essay '*The Crucible* in History', he discusses what he saw as the mood of the 1950s, and admits that it was partly his horror of what he saw that led him to write *The Crucible* as a means of both conveying his anger at such proceedings and exposing the collateral damage they caused. Connecting McCarthyism to the way people acted in Salem, Miller felt that the 1950s American vision of communism was a moral issue, which viewed communists as in league with the Devil. This he linked to the Puritan sense of rectitude, that seemed to suggest that anyone with whom they disagreed must be allied to Satan.

Miller initially resisted the idea of depicting the HUAC hearings in the form of an old-fashioned witch trial as too obvious. However, as the HUAC hearings grew more ritualistic and cruelly pointless, he could no longer resist, despite the obvious risks, for the parallels were far too apt to ignore. He saw how both sets of hearings had a definite structure behind them, designed to make people publicly confess. In both cases the 'judges' knew in advance all of the information for which they asked. The main difference was that Salem's hearings had a greater legality as it was against the law to be a witch, but it was not illegal to be a communist in 1950s America. Miller does not attempt a one-to-one analogy between his characters and those involved in HUAC, because this would have made the play too immediately paradigmatic and temporal. Miller himself appeared before HUAC three years after he wrote *The Crucible*. Summoned before a group of hostile and opportunistic politicians he presented a speech that virtually echoed that of John Proctor, in which he, too, refused to name names or bring trouble on anyone else. Miller was convicted of contempt, but his lawyer was able to get his one-year sentence reduced to the suspension of a single month and a $500 fine. Rather than accept a conviction that represented wrongdoing, Miller appealed. By August the following year the conviction was overturned by the United States Court of Appeals on the grounds that the questions that he had been asked served no legislative purpose.

Miller insisted that while McCarthyism may have informed *The Crucible*, it is not its major theme. We never go inside the courtroom, because Miller is not interested in the proceedings as much as the motivations behind them, and the fears and reactions of those involved. The play's continued success depends on the realisation that it offers more than a straightforward history lesson of either HUAC or the witch trials. Rather, *The Crucible* explores the prevailing conditions that precipitate such events. This allows Miller's play a continuing resonance as historical conditions of persecution, intolerance and sanctimonious denunciation continue to repeat themselves in a variety of political and historical circumstances. *The Crucible* speaks to every conflict between an individual conscience and tyranny, whether it is the tyranny of religion, government,

race, economics or simply that of public opinion.
Connections to past and present injustices and periods of
overly zealous patriotism or fundamentalist fervour find
their resonance in this work. Miller viewed the right-wing
attacks on President Clinton over the Lewinsky Affair as
redolent of the Salem magistrates attacking the accused
while revelling in the potent sexual details of a supposed
allegiance to the Devil; and directing the play in 2006,
Dominic Cooke saw parallels to 'Bush and Blair generating
hysteria over terrorism and the frightening rise of Christian
Fundamentalism in the US'.

The play's theatrical context and place in Miller's oeuvre
While the extensive notes that Miller added to his script
may recall the social earnestness of George Bernard Shaw,
The Crucible follows an American theatrical tradition,
advanced by the agitprop plays of the 1930s, of drama that
seriously addresses key social and political issues. Miller's
outspokenness against such dangerous manifestations as
McCarthyism, encoded within the play, was the kind of
moral stance that made Miller so admired by both
contemporary and subsequent playwrights. His theatrical
goal was to appeal to the best instincts of the society for
which he wrote.
    Not as formally innovative or experimental as *Death of a
Salesman* or *After the Fall*, *The Crucible* can be viewed as one of
Miller's more realistic pieces. Like his earlier *All My Sons*, it
has strong connections to the social realism of Henrik Ibsen,
in which earlier indiscretions return to haunt the protagonist
as 'the chickens come home to roost'. Just prior to *The
Crucible*, Miller adapted Ibsen's *An Enemy of the People*, and
that play's central character, Dr Thomas Stockmann, shares
something of the moral authority of John Proctor.
    Miller viewed *The Crucible* as a companion piece to *Death
of a Salesman* in the way both plays explore the role of the
individual in conflict with the dictates of society. Having
argued in 1949 that tragedy could be written about the
common man, in *The Crucible* Miller presents us with

another working-class tragic protagonist whose actions are partly determined by forces outside himself. However, unlike Willy Loman, Proctor exhibits a greater degree of conscience, and ends with a better understanding of himself and the events around him. For Miller art has only been useful when it tries to change society for the better, and *The Crucible* is the play he wrote which is most clearly informed by that sense of purpose. The play's ability to span the distance from 1692 Salem to contemporary times allows for a study of the nature of America herself, with some striking lessons. Miller raises disturbing questions about the function of authority and the rights of the individual that speak to people who have never even heard of Salem or McCarthyism. It is this wide-ranging aspect that gives the play its theatrical appeal.

Although the work's initial reception was lukewarm, partly due to its controversial political analogy, *The Crucible* cemented Miller's reputation as one of America's foremost playwrights, and it has grown to become Miller's most resilient play. Its popularity is due both to its craft, which makes it a solid choice for stage production, and the widely applicable aspects of its subject and theme, which continue to fascinate audiences throughout the world. The large cast, including a number of parts for young female players, has made it a staple of school, college and community theatre, along with its frequent presence on academic syllabuses both on the secondary school and university level. *The Crucible* has become the most produced drama in the Miller repertory, and, after Thornton Wilder's *Our Town*, the most performed of any American drama.

The principal themes

Individualism vs. community
In the spring of 1692, Salem was a recently founded, religiously devout township, a communal society, it was supported by an autocratic theocracy to help it attain the discipline necessary for survival. Its inhabitants were

suspicious of individuality because they saw it as a threat to the imposed sense of order. Authority, and obedience to that authority, had long defined their lives. Constantly threatened by the surrounding wilderness, Salemites worked hard to survive. Their way of life was strict and sombre, with dancing and frivolity frowned upon as wasteful. Concentrating on survival left them little opportunity to misbehave. Ironically, although their families had come to America to avoid persecution, they became intolerant, constantly judging each other's behaviour. The witch trials offered them a release of pent-up frustration and emotion. Under the guise of morality they were given the opportunity to take vengeance on neighbours towards whom they felt envy or hostility. Growing family sizes had led to disputes over property rights, and the fact that anyone accused of witchcraft would have had their lands forfeited either to a claimant or the Church gave many the opportunity, like the Putnams, increase their holdings by making accusations.

The Crucible explores how societies define themselves, the dangers inherent in this process, especially to the individual, and the nature of power itself. Given Miller's democratic views, he is fearful of the consequences of allowing too few too much power, largely because, given natural human weakness, it is all too easy for those few to put their private interest before the common good. The play depicts a conflict between individualism and community, with a single conscience pitted against the weight of a social authority that has been corrupted by selfishness and hypocrisy. We see in the actions of the prosecutors, the blindness that results from paranoia and inflexible belief. The drama illustrates how an entrenched system leads to a desire to negate the opinions of others. What results is a totalitarian social structure where those with a voice, given to them by a financial or political standing, effectively silence dissent. Such societies become intolerant of individual thinkers who question or refuse to accept all they are told to believe. The Proctors are already partly damned by their scepticism over the presence of witches and their refusal to kowtow to a venal minister, both of which make them easy targets.

Miller demonstrates how social forces operate on people, in part to show the falsity of our belief in individual human autonomy. Total freedom, he suggests, is largely a myth in any working society. The actions of Proctor and others in the play are partially dictated by forces beyond themselves, which demand of them sacrifices they have little choice but to make. While Proctor, Rebecca, Martha and Elizabeth stand trial individually, the refusal to confess or name others is as much dictated by a social conscience as a personal one. The ideal would be a balance between the desires of the individual and the needs of the community, but this is a hard balance to attain, especially in a hierarchical society such as the one developed in Salem, where the few are given power over the many.

From the Putnams, to Parris, to the trial judges, *The Crucible* depicts how the unscrupulous can declare the presence of evil to cripple whoever disagrees with them, not just religiously, but politically and socially. They assume a moral high ground, so anyone who disagrees is deemed immoral and damned, without recourse to defence. Tituba and the children were trying to commune with dark forces, but if left alone their exploits would have bothered no one – their actions an indication of how young people react against social and sexual repression. A community stays strong by allowing its individual members some measure of autonomy; when any society becomes too restrictive, trouble is bound to ensue.

Guilt and responsibility

The Greek playwrights and Henrik Ibsen were strong influences on Miller from the beginning of his career. Both wrote plays in which past mistakes inevitably impinge on the present. Miller was interested in the role guilt might play in such circumstances, and how characters deal with guilt is a common theme in much of his work. Earlier plays, such as *All My Sons* or *Death of a Salesman*, have narrative arcs that lead to the uncovering of a literal or moral crime, at which point they end. In the character of Proctor, Miller wanted to move beyond the discovery of guilt to a more circumstantial study of its effects. What follows in this case is an exploration of how guilt can be transformed into responsibility.

In *The Crucible* Miller explores what happens when people allow others to be the judge of their conscience. Through Proctor, Miller examines the conflict between a person's deeds and that person's conception of himself. Proctor is presented as a man caught between the way in which others see him and the way he sees himself. He has betrayed his wife, ruined a young girl, and feels he must pay for his indiscretion. His private sense of guilt leads him to make a false confession for a crime of which he is patently innocent, although he later recants. What allows him to recant is the release of guilt given to him by his wife's admission of her coldness and her refusal to blame him for his adultery. Elizabeth insists that he is a good man, which finally convinces him that he is. This allows him to accept his death rather than 'confess' and damage the reputation of others, which would return him to a guilt he can no longer accept. His death is less atonement for any earlier sin than a martyrdom to help the people of Salem regain their sanity. Thus he transforms his personal guilt into a wider responsibility for others.

Marriage

The Crucible dramatises a debate on the theme of marriage, and what a marriage requires to make it work. At the time of writing the play Miller, a father of two and married to Mary Slattery, was considering an affair with Marilyn Monroe. It is unsurprising, then, to find the issue of marriage explored. The director Elia Kazan introduced him to Monroe in 1951 while the two were in Hollywood to find a film producer for *The Hook*, but Miller resisted her temptations, returning to New York to try and patch up his already failing marriage. His confession to Slattery put a further strain on their relationship. While he dedicated the play 'To Mary', and hopefully depicted a couple who were able to transcend a past indiscretion, his own marriage did not last. Unlike Elizabeth Proctor, Mary took no blame upon herself and their relationship remained strained. In 1955 Monroe came to New York and began her relationship with Miller, which led to his divorce from Slattery and subsequent marriage to Monroe.

The Proctors' marriage lies at the play's centre, and the love triangle Miller creates between Abigail and the Proctors echoes his own. But just as the play transcends its historical basis, it also goes beyond the autobiographical. Issues of trust, love and what a partner owes the other are discussed in a number of scenes. It is Giles Corey's idle tongue and distrust of his wife that contribute to getting her hanged, while Francis Nurse staunchly defends his wife even at risk of being found in contempt.

Proctor and Elizabeth profoundly love each other, but seven months before the play begins, while his wife was sick, he had an affair with their serving girl, Abigail. We do not know how long this might have continued had not Elizabeth discovered her husband's adultery, but Proctor insists it was nothing more than animal passion. Abigail is sent away, but the trust between the married couple has shattered, and all ease between them is gone. Insecure about her own attractiveness, Elizabeth looks for signs that her husband continues to stray. Tortured by guilt over what he sees as a moment of weakness, Proctor vacillates between apologetic attempts to make his wife happy and anger at her continued distrust. It is not until both suffer at the hands of the court that they come to an understanding of each other and their mutual love. Each is willing to sacrifice everything for the sake of the other. Proctor tries to free Elizabeth by ruining his own name with a public confession of adultery, while she lies for the first and only time in her life to save him. Their final scene together is deeply touching, as we see Elizabeth declare her love, and willingness to sacrifice that love, by allowing Proctor to die rather than relinquish his integrity. The re-establishment of trust between them is made evident when Proctor regains a sense of his own worth by accepting his wife's vision of him as a good man.

Sex and religion

The dangers of orthodoxy and desire are part of a discussion through which Miller represents the puritanical fear of sex. The girls go to the dark woods to indulge in their sexual fantasies, as they are given no room to do so in a fiercely restricted society. Sexual repression within this puritanical community is revealed to be a major factor in the troubles that ensue. It is also a determining factor in the behaviour of many of the play's characters.

Puritanism coloured every aspect of how the people of Salem lived. This meant giving full obedience to the Church – each man, woman and child was expected to attend services each week. Sermons were measured by hours, often full of references to hellfire, and inattention was scorned. Puritans felt chosen by God for a special purpose; He would be watching every moment, so discipline was imperative. Discipline of others and of the self, and anything that threatened that discipline, would be scrupulously observed. Salem believed in both the Devil and the existence of witches, and felt under constant threat from both. Obedience to the Church and its dictates would help keep them safe.

For the people of Salem, Satan was alive and nearby in the dark forest. Miller allows the forest to act as a representation of hell, to be avoided at the cost of sin. The main sin is sex, which has been notoriously equated with the Devil by the Christian view of original sin. While godly folk stay at home at night, the girls dance illicitly in the woods around a fire (another hellish symbol), with Mercy naked and Abigail drinking blood to cast a spell on Elizabeth. Desire makes them wicked. Abigail's bedevilment is reinforced by the symbols that surround her: she has been initiated into the temptation of sex by her former employer through her 'sense for heat' and still feels Proctor 'burning' for her. He is described in his adulterous lust as a 'stallion', a beast that acts without self-control.

A central irony of the play is that by fixating so much on sin, the religious right, represented by Parris and Danforth, become sinful and 'turned' from God. Proctor accuses Parris of preaching too much 'hellfire and bloody damnation' and saying too little about God; this becomes a kind of prophesy as Parris and the judges become increasingly devilish in their treatment of others, condemning innocent people to death on spurious evidence. Signing the death warrants becomes an issue of pride rather than belief. As Proctor suggests when he is arrested, the fires of hell will consume the supposedly righteous for their 'black hearts' rather than the 'guilty' witches.

Gender and race
When people are treated by different standards in any society, dangers ensue. Both the gender and racial inequality are depicted in *The Crucible*, and without the confession of the slave Tituba and the outcry of the young girls, the subsequent horrors of the Salem witch trials might have been avoided. Therefore, what motivated these female figures becomes an important factor in our understanding of such occurrences.

The fact that most of the accused were female is dramatically significant. Women of that era were believed to be weaker and more lustful than men, and therefore more susceptible to temptation from the Devil. Although wives were given some authority in running the home, the husband was considered the undisputed head of the household. This is perhaps why Proctor resents the fact that his wife will not forgive him. Kept under double submission, both to men and God, strong-willed women would not have had easy lives. Growing up, boys had many more outlets beyond the home, being allowed to explore in order to fish and hunt. Girls were expected to tend the house, and were encouraged to be subservient. Disobedient children were swiftly disciplined and taught to obey. Even lower in the hierarchy than children would be anyone who was not white. Tituba is never allowed to defend herself from the accusations brought against her, but simply assumed to be guilty because of the colour of her skin, which her accusers believe automatically allies her with the Devil. They ignore her protestations of faith, and force her either to confess or die, which is little choice at all.

The girls of the town are similarly bullied. Several adults (including Proctor) suggest beating as a punishment for untoward behaviour – a common treatment at the time for any infringement of the rules. Young, unmarried servant girls are considered chattels rather than viable members of the community, ordered to and fro and chastised if they display any sign of independent thought. They were allowed to make no decisions for themselves, and were given no avenue to gain respect outside of marriage. The patriarchal Salem authorities may represent order and security, but such an arrangement comes at a heavy price. It is a price not all the girls are prepared to pay, hence their nocturnal visits to the forest, the place of the unknown and freedom from the town's restrictions.

In the forest the girls danced as their spirits and desires ran free; it is no wonder they found such escapades exciting. They carried this freedom forwards into the courtroom, where for the first time they are shown respect, as Abigail leads them to cry out against many of the town's elders. But such actions become a dangerous threat to the community. Introducing a form of chaos into a tightly ordered society, their actions go against everything this society holds sacred. Parris's fear that Abigail and her friends are going into the woods at night to dance naked and invoke the Devil is therefore justified, for by so doing they are attacking the foundations of their society: its religious beliefs, its social conventions and the sanctity of marriage (as Abigail plots to take Elizabeth's life and replace her). When a society consistently restricts an individual and will not allow a person to show independence or individuality, it effectively destroys the individual's spirit. The question arises as to whether or not we can condone the actions of an individual who tries to break a community's status quo.

It is hard to believe that Miller intends us to view Abigail – a young, orphaned girl who has been seduced by her boss (an older, family man and respected member of his society) and deflowered in an age when virginity was a prerequisite for marriage – as a villain. Indeed, from a feminist perspective she becomes increasingly sympathetic. After such treatment she is thrown out of the house on orders from the man's wife, and forced to live with her petulant and demanding uncle. She tries to win back Proctor's affection, resorting to casting spells on his wife to remove her from the competition. When she meets him again, she declares her love, but is ignored and rejected. He even threatens to disgrace her in the town. It is not until he publicly confesses their relationship that she finally attacks him, which could be viewed as an attempt to protect herself rather than a malicious act of revenge. Can we condemn such a girl, as the men of the play do, as a wanton whore? Even the wronged wife insists, 'There is a promise made in any bed', and admits the girl might indeed love her husband.

To view John Proctor as an innocent who has been seduced by an evil whore is too easy. Abigail is in love with Proctor, and it may be that he still harbours feelings for her. When she declares, 'You loved me, John Proctor, and whatever sin it is, you love me yet!' he does not deny the charge. Having been awakened by her affair from a slumbering servitude to see her potential as a human being, Abigail struggles to uncover a sense of self in a highly restrictive society. She creates for herself a position of respect outside of marriage by becoming the voice of accusation which all fear, a role more traditionally held by males who hold every position of authority. She refuses to accept a patriarchal society that silences and denounces independent, female vitality. She justifies the victimisation of her fellow women by calling them hypocrites who, like the men, have tried to keep her in her place. Her gulling of the judges, and eventual escape with the mercenary Parris's savings before the town turns against her, might depict her as victorious – a woman who refuses to be controlled and who wins her freedom through her own quick thinking. As a sad reflection of the lack of opportunities open to women in those times, however, we eventually learn that she ends up as a prostitute in Boston.

Key elements of style

While Miller never intended to present an historically accurate depiction of the Salem witch trials, having made several changes for 'dramatic purposes', he did view his depiction as an 'honest' one. He wanted his audience to be drawn into the world he created, but felt the archaic speech of the period might be off-putting. He developed his own poetic language for the play, based on the language he had read in Salem documents. Wanting to make his audience feel they were witnessing events from an earlier time, yet not wanting to make the dialogue incomprehensible, he devised a form of speech for his characters that blended into present-day speech an earlier vocabulary and syntax. Incorporating more familiar archaic words like 'yea', 'nay', or 'goodly', Miller created the impression of a past era without distancing his audience from the action.

The play's language, however, is complex nonetheless, as it offers itself as a study in the power of the spoken and written word. It shows how accusations, once voiced in public, tend to stick, however much they are denied. We can view *The Crucible* as an exploration of how Salem performed its witch trials in the same way as we might watch a play. The trials were public events and, like the HUAC hearings, became show trials in which the guilt or innocence of those accused became less important than how the judges and accusers 'acted'. As Danforth complains when asked to delay the executions, 'Postponement now speaks a floundering on my part.' It is a performance in which those in power are in the director's seat and can choose how they wish to interpret what they hear. To write such things down gives them even greater power. Proctor recognises this when he is asked to write down his confession as well as voice it. There is an authority given to the written word that prevents ambiguity.

The fact that the first draft of the play was written in verse and later broken down into prose reflects in Miller's frequent use of poetic imagery within the deceptively simple speech patterns of his characters. Although this is one of

Miller's more realistic plays, it is based on a central and controlling metaphor. A 'crucible' subjects items to great heat in order to purify their nature – the condition faced by the central characters of Proctor, Elizabeth and Hale. All endure intense suffering to emerge as more morally secure and more self-aware individuals. Miller also incorporates images of heat and light against cold and dark to play against our common concepts of heaven and hell and good and evil. Numerous references to cold and winter and the hardness of stone are used to indicate the harshness of Puritan life, trapped as it is in a cycle of toil unrelieved by leisure, as they strive to tame the hard landscape and their own natural impulses within the mandates of a restrictive religion. Abigail tells John that he is 'no wintry man', which is true in that he refuses to abide by many of the strictures of his community and is determined to have a mind of his own. It is partly this independent spirit that makes him such an obvious target. The network of symbolic elements within the play – from the 'crucible' of the title to the woods surrounding the township as well as the extended metaphors regarding blood, fire and ice – all contribute to the play's rich and unexpected lyricism.

The characters

John Proctor

Although the original John Proctor was not a major figure in the Salem trials, Miller makes him the central protagonist. In his mid-thirties, Proctor is a straightforward man of common sense who is impatient with foolishness in others. This has at times led him into trouble with neighbours who dislike his bluntness, and will lead him into further trouble with the court, which views his scepticism as undermining their authority. A freer thinker than many of the townspeople, Proctor does not believe in witches and has a relatively egalitarian outlook for a Puritan, to the point where Parris accuses him of acting like a Quaker. Quakers were far less rigid than the Puritans and, to Parris's mind, less scrupulous in their religious devotion. Despite his relative openness, Proctor remains a strong disciplinarian – as most Puritan heads of family would have been – and is prepared to beat his servants. He expects his wife to forgive him once he has confessed. Despite his lapse with Abigail, he is a moral man, he works hard, values his friends and feels guilt over his shortcomings. Proctor's view of Reverend Parris as an ungodly materialist, and his subsequent refusal to attend church or have his third son baptised, show him as a man of principle. But this is exactly what works against him.

Miller describes Proctor as a sinner not just in the general sense 'but against his own vision of decent conduct' – in other words, he has become his own harshest critic. He fully repents of his weakness for Abigail, and Miller expects us to forgive him this lapse even if he cannot do so himself. Despite his adultery, he feels his commitment to his marriage deeply, which is why he confesses to Elizabeth and tries to make amends. Abigail has been sent away and he has vowed to have nothing more to do with her, a vow he has not found easy to uphold, but one he has kept. Elizabeth, we are told, is pregnant, which tells us that the couple continues to have sexual relations despite Elizabeth's disappointment in him. He tries hard to please his wife and be a better husband and father, and he does all he can to save her after her arrest, even going so far as to sacrifice himself.

Miller wants his hero to be realistic and he shows him with his human flaws. He is a man of deep passion, which not only led him into an affair with his servant, but can also be observed in the intensity of his frustration and anger. His rocky relationship with Elizabeth highlights this passion: one moment he is deeply solicitous, the next furiously angry. His attitude towards women often borders on the dictatorial; enlightened though he is, he is still a man of his time, and these were times in which the man was the head of his own household. There are moments when he seems unable to control his temper both verbally and physically. Shouting 'God is dead', and declaring the judges damned at his arrest, he also tears up the warrant for Elizabeth's arrest and makes physical threats against both Mary and Abigail.

His anger seems rooted in an awareness that these events are partly his fault; if he had left Abigail alone, she might never have been driven to such lengths. Angry with himself for having betrayed his wife, he almost makes a false confession of witchcraft, in one sense to punish himself for what he has done. Once Proctor controls his anger, however, he is able to act in a far more positive fashion. His ultimate refusal to go along with the confession indicates his awareness that he has a responsibility to himself and his community. He would rather hang than participate in the false judgment of others. Through Proctor and the others who die with him, Miller acknowledges the heroism of these victims in order to recognise and celebrate the existence of such personal integrity even in the bleakest of worlds.

Elizabeth Proctor
Elizabeth begins the play hurt by and suspicious of her husband, having discovered his adultery seven months before. Though Abigail has been dismissed, they have all kept the real reason secret. Elizabeth's pregnancy could be as much the result of an adherence to a religious imperative to procreate as it is an indication of a fixed and renewed relationship. Indeed, she seems to have forgiven little and is both angry and distant, even while she performs her household duties. Elizabeth's apparent acceptance of events might lead us to judge her as merely a compliant wife, but she has both spirit and strength. Elizabeth acted decisively on hearing about her husband's affair, sending Abigail away and forcing Proctor to atone. It is also Elizabeth who pushes Proctor to denounce Abigail, as she fears that Abigail might act against her. Her forceful response on hearing that Abigail's 'poppet' has set the scene for her arrest ('She must be ripped out of the world') reminds us that she, too, has the human potential for violence.

Displaying great strength of character, she stands up to Hale on a number of occasions; even her husband's response is more deferential. Hurt by Hale's accusations, she denies that good people could become agents of the

Devil and announces, 'If you think that I am [a witch], then I say there are none.' Bravely, she allows herself to be taken to jail rather than cause fruitless fighting. She quietly counters both Hale and Danforth as they try to manipulate her into forcing her husband to confess and promises 'nothing'. The dry eyes that Danforth takes as signs of her unnaturalness represent her strength and understanding in the face of their inflexibility. Although her pregnancy has saved her for the time being from being hanged with the rest, she is no less firm in her refusal to confess. Her dignity is further underlined by her acceptance of her husband's decision to be hanged at the play's close. Her love for Proctor is never greater than when she allows him to die.

Elizabeth's love and respect for her husband, although it has been severely tested by his adultery, is displayed when she lies for him in front of Danforth. She is a woman of staunch faith, to whom a lie would be a cardinal sin, yet she lies to save him embarrassment or worse. In Puritan times adultery carried harsh punishment for both participants. It is ironic that it is this lie that condemns him in the eyes of the judges. Her suffering in jail causes her to reflect on her former treatment of Proctor, and in their final meeting she confesses she has been cold towards him in the past. She recognises the part she has played in driving him into the arms of Abigail, and insists on her husband's essential goodness. It is this belief that strengthens Proctor to chose a dignified death rather than an ignoble betrayal by signing his name to a false document.

Abigail Williams
In her character description we are told that Abigail has 'an endless capacity for dissembling', which should prepare us for her vagrant allegiances and ability to manipulate others. We might have sympathy for a young orphaned girl whose parents were killed in front of her, whose only relative is a self-concerned minister, who lost her virginity to an older man while still in her teens and was then tossed aside. However, given the damage she causes to others in Salem it

is difficult not to view Abigail as wicked, despite the
circumstances that might have led her to behave in the way
she does.

In the original Salem account Abigail was only eleven
years old, but Miller increased her age to allow for her affair
with Proctor. Abigail is the most complex of the girls of the
town who cry out against their elders. Both clever and
cunning, her cynicism about the so-called respectability of
the town is partly supported by the way we see them act.
Her understanding of people's darker sides – she sees no one
as free of corruption and selfish motivation – allows her to
be very manipulative, and she can even stand up to a figure
like Danforth. While Danforth is an upholder of the rules,
she is the exact opposite, a total anarchist who refuses to
play by any other rules.

Abigail was awakened to her sexuality by her brief affair
with Proctor, and is no longer content to play the role of
meek serving girl. She sees in Proctor someone who treated
her as a woman rather than a childish nuisance. Her desire
for him seems to transcend the physical, and she has
magnified the importance he holds in her life beyond any
reasonable expectation. An additional scene, which Miller
wrote to feature Abigail and Proctor, shows her uneasy
psychological state, a result of her irrepressible desire for
Proctor. She believes she is being attacked by the spirits of
those she has had convicted. She quickly recovers her
stability by Act Three, as she faces up to Danforth and forces
the judges to overlook Proctor's charges of her corruption by
manipulating Mary to accuse him of witchcraft.

Abigail uses the town's superstitious leanings to her own
advantage, to claim greater respect in the community and
revenge herself upon Elizabeth, who has 'blackened' her
name with her dismissal and kept her from Proctor. The
way she sacrifices former friends like Tituba to the court,
without care, suggests her amorality. She will turn on her
beloved Proctor in an act of self-preservation, and when the
possibility of rebellion arises, she quickly flees, stealing
Parris's savings on the way. Her fate as a prostitute in
Boston seems almost inevitable.

Reverend Samuel Parris

In his mid-forties, Reverend Parris is the current minister of Salem, and anxious to keep his post. As the third minister Salem has hired in seven years, he wants to ensure he is not so easily dismissed, and ingratiates himself with those who have power, the Putnams and Danforth. Before being ordained he had been in business in Barbados, and this worldly background dictates how he now runs his ministry, wrangling for higher pay and the deeds to his house. He has estranged honest men like John Proctor because of his materialism and concentration on negative aspects of their common religion. He preaches so much 'hellfire and bloody damnation' that people are reluctant to bring their children to church. He considers any dissension from his views as both personal persecution and an attack on the Church itself.

There is no one in the play, including the judges, who respects Parris. Danforth has little patience with him and Hathorne considers him unbalanced. As a minister of God he strikes an ungodly figure, being petulant, selfish, unmerciful and awkward in his relationships with others, especially children. A widower, he has little interest in children and is clearly at a loss as to how to treat his own daughter. Parris's first thought on learning of his daughter's bewitching is how it affects him and his standing in the community. He would be prepared, also, to condemn his niece, Abigail, rather than allow her reputation to sully his by association. He is more reticent than the Putnams in bringing forward charges of witchcraft, even withholding information about what he saw the girls doing in the woods, but this is because of his own insecurity rather than any concern over endangering innocent lives.

Despite his initial doubts, it is Parris who brings in the witchfinders to ensure he keeps people like the Putnams content. He soon becomes a staunch advocate of condemning everyone the girls name, without allowing any proper defence. Indeed, he is the first to charge any defence as an attempt to undermine the court, including Proctor's efforts to defame Abigail, about whom he had previously had strong suspicions. His treatment of his slave, Tituba, who has raised his child for him and served him for many years, is savage in the extreme; threatening to whip her to death if she does not immediately confess, which allows her little option but to do so. Her declaration that the Devil has told her to cut his throat because he is 'no goodly man' but a 'mean man and no gentle man' indicates how he has most likely treated her for much of her service. As final proof of his self-regard, Parris turns against the idea of the witch trials only when his own life is threatened and he begins to fear rebellion. He helps Hale pray with the condemned to persuade them to confess, only to prove he was right – Hale, by contrast, is trying to save lives.

Reverend John Hale
The Reverend John Hale comes from Beverly, a nearby town, where in the previous year he thought he had found a witch who cast a spell over a young girl, but this turned out to be a mere case of neglect. Nearing forty, he is well-read, and has a reputation for understanding the demonic arts, so Parris has called him to Salem to investigate the rumours of witchcraft. Hale truly believes that witches exist and he is disturbed when the Proctors express their doubts. Beginning the play as a self-regarding, even a conceited, figure, Hale sees himself as superior to the people of Salem; he is determined to uncover the villagers' evil spirits. As the girls' accusations begin to fall upon upright members of the community, Hale's convictions are eroded by doubt.

   Once set in motion, the juggernaut of the trials cannot be stopped by Hale's growing concern for truth, yet his resistance helps to expose the flaws in the judges' closed logical system when he questions their motives. In contrast to the other judges, Hale shows himself to be more rational and conscientious by honestly considering the evidence. His private interviews with Rebecca and Elizabeth convey his growing doubts, while his assurance to the Proctors that Rebecca's goodness is self-evident just before we get news of her arrest shows us how little influence he actually has.

Recognising the deception of the girls, he denounces the proceedings and tries to save the victims, but soon recognises the futility of his stance. Urging people he knows are innocent to confess in order to save their lives, he becomes a lost figure, not knowing what to believe, unable to understand the Proctors' noble behaviour in provoking the court to hang a truly innocent man.

The judges

One of the judges brought in from Boston, Judge Hathorne is described as a 'bitter, remorseless' man, and he is certainly more concerned with his own power than he is with uncovering the truth. His refusal to listen to others makes him contemptible. He has chosen to believe the girls and will allow nothing to shake that belief; any evidence brought to challenge this is viewed as necessarily false. He defers to Danforth, recognising his greater power, but insists on finding those accused guilty, even if it means harassing inconvenient witnesses like Mary to undermine their credibility. Giles's comment, 'You're not a Boston judge yet, Hathorne', suggests that Hathorne is an ambitious man whose involvement here is designed to advance his career on a higher court in Boston, rather than to uncover the truth in Salem.

However contemptible Hathorne appears to be, Deputy-Governor Danforth is even worse. He is more sophisticated than his fellow judges, which makes him more dangerous. Miller has described him as the 'rule-bearer' of the play who guards boundaries strictly because he cannot cope with the potential chaos caused by free thought. He is loath to relinquish control to anyone and forcefully dominates his fellow judges. Although he listens to counter-arguments, it is not with an open mind, and when he hangs the condemned with full knowledge of their innocence we should recognise him as an evil force. He places his own reputation above innocent lives and uses religion to justify the deceit. Danforth is as intelligent and strong-willed as Proctor, and becomes his main antagonist. Unlike

Proctor, however, he is unwilling to change. He is responsible for putting four hundred people in jail throughout the area and he has sentenced seventy-two of them to hang. His proud announcement of these facts to Giles suggests he enjoys power and views himself as superior to those he judges.

Judges Stoughton and Sewall are mentioned as being in the court, but we never see them on stage. In the 1996 movie version Miller gives Judge Sewall a larger role, and portrays him as one judge who is less certain that what they are doing is right; this allows for an even greater case against Danforth.

Thomas and Ann Putnam

Although one of the richest men in the town, Thomas Putnam is a sour man filled with grievances against others, that have been created mostly by his own imagination and sense of self-importance. Greedy and argumentative, Putnam is not above manipulating truth and law to his own vindictive ends, and he may even have persuaded his daughter, Ruth, to cry out against men whose lands he covets. He argues with John Proctor over who owns a tract of land bearing timber, and he has had similar arguments with many other of the town's landowners, including the Nurses. A bitter man, he has even tried to break his father's will because he disagreed with the amount that had been left to a stepbrother. This was another public failure, which has embittered him further against the town. One genuine grievance, however, is against those Salemites who stood in the way of the appointment of his wife's brother-in-law, James Bradley, to the post of minister. Bradley had been well-qualified and had a majority of votes, but a small faction within the town, including the Nurses, managed to block his selection. Putnam believes his family honour has been belittled. In revenge, Putnam arranged for the minister who obtained the post, George Burroughs, to be sent to jail for debts he had not actually owed. It is little wonder that Parris wants to keep Putnam satisfied.

Ann Putnam is no less self-absorbed and vindictive, though for a religious woman she ascribes far too much value to superstition. Like her husband, she assumes that everyone else is plotting against her. It is she who sent her daughter into the woods to persuade Tituba to conjure a spell to explain why she has lost so many children. In Salem infant mortality was high and her loss of seven babies, although unfortunate, would not have been so unusual for the period. In their self-opinionated and self-serving rectitude, the Putnams represent the worst face of Puritanism.

Giles and Martha Corey

Eighty-three years old, but still a 'powerful' man, Giles Corey is an argumentative figure who fights with his neighbours and frequently takes them to court. Proctor tells us that he paid a fine to Giles for slandering him even though he had said nothing, but they remain friends, helping each other with the harder farmwork. Unlike Putnam, who appears malicious in his dealings, Giles's wrangling makes him comic and indicates his independent spirit. Giles has the courage and strength of the pioneer stock from which he sprang. He has married Martha late in life and only then became religious, so it is little wonder he stumbles over his prayers. At heart he is a good man, and he dies for his beliefs no less bravely than John Proctor. His refusal to speak as they weigh him down with rocks until he dies means that the authorities cannot confiscate his lands as they can those charged or condemned.

His wife, Martha, whom we briefly hear offstage but never see, seems a decent woman and is clearly no witch. Her interest in books indicates a lively mind rather than allegiance to the Devil. She is charged with witchcraft by a fellow townsperson to whom she had sold a pig which later died from neglect. The man has been unable to keep pigs since, most likely for the same reasons, but takes out his frustration by blaming Martha. Several townspeople vouch for her, but they too are arrested, and since she refuses to confess to being in league with the Devil, she is hanged alongside Proctor.

Francis and Rebecca Nurse

Town elders Rebecca and Francis Nurse offer a kinder picture of Puritanism than that depicted by the Putnams. Francis Nurse is the opposite of Thomas Putnam, being a man who puts others before himself, living a truly moral life. He is genuinely shocked by Danforth's reaction to the document he has had his friends sign in support of his wife, never wanting to bring trouble on anyone else. He has been the town's unofficial judge up to this point, evidence of his probity. He never sought this position, but it has made him and his family targets for those of a jealous nature. Many of the town's older families, such as the Putnams, resent the prosperity of the Nurses, seeing them as upstarts.

Francis's wife, Rebecca, is the ideal Puritan, who lives her faith, always showing kindness and compassion to others and displaying a gentleness in her life which is rightly respected – she can calm Betty by her mere presence. It is no wonder so many Salem people risk themselves by vouching for her. But she has a powerful enemy in Ann Putnam, who is jealous that Rebecca had eleven healthy children and lots of grandchildren, while seven of her own babies died. Ann accuses her of murder, and it is a sign of the times that the court even considers such a charge. It is her arrest and conviction that lead Hale to doubt the validity of the accusations. Rebecca is rightly horrified that Proctor endangers his soul by offering false testimony and never wavers in her refusal to co-operate with the court, going to her death with the same dignity with which she has lived.

Tituba and Sarah Good

Tituba and Sarah Good confess to witchcraft rather than hang, and they are readily believed, as neither has a good reputation in the town. The first people arrested were of a similar standing, which is why Salem went along with the judges' decisions. Sarah Good is a drunkard and a vagrant, and as a foreigner who is racially different Tituba has already been judged by the township to have an allegiance to dark forces. Tituba shows more personal concern for Betty Parris than Betty's father and she seems a decent woman. Though an adult, the colour of her skin and consequent low standing in the town have made her less of a threat to the girls, and they have been more open with her than with other adults. She has used her cultural knowledge to assist their requests for potions and charms, but with no sense of any allegiance to the Devil. However, her denials fall on deaf ears as Parris and Hale treat her as if she had already confessed. It is ironic that a woman who began the play asserting her allegiance to Christianity should end calling to the Devil. It is an indication of the true nature of the trials which have driven her to this, a connection Proctor makes when he asserts, 'I hear the boot of Lucifer, I see his filthy face.'

The girls
Mercy Lewis, Susanna Walcott, Betty Parris, Ruth Putnam and Mary Warren are among the young girls who follow Abigail's lead. All have led lives of limited possibility up until this point, as they have been bullied by employers, forced to be quiet and subservient. The only freedom they have had is sneaking off to the woods with the only person in town of a lower social standing than theirs: the black slave, Tituba. We see with Mary how harsh even good people like the Proctors are with their servant girls, restricting what they can do and whipping them when they fail in their service.

   Mercy seems the closest in spirit to Abigail; she goes naked in the woods and is attracted by what she sees as Proctor's masculinity. She is clearly a girl who wants more than the quiet, restricted town of Salem can offer. Abigail allows the girls a chance to be at the centre of attention and treated as special. They are attracted to the power they see themselves holding over the townspeople when they offer the judges any names they like. We see Mary grow more independent with the understanding that her employers can no longer treat her with disdain.

Each girl is drawn into the plot for slightly different reasons, though many stay involved out of fear of what Abigail might do next. Ruth Putnam is doing this for her father, so he can grab the land of the accused, but Betty and Mary are simpler souls and seem drawn in against their wills by group hysteria. Betty's initial coma indicates her timid nature, literally paralysed as she is by having been caught doing something she knows is wrong. Mary, who has been used by Abigail to implicate Elizabeth with the possession of the 'voodoo' poppet, tries to tell the truth, but she is isolated and afraid once Abigail has the other girls gang up against her. Uneasy in conflict, Mary has been from the start the weakest of the group. She only watched in the woods and was not directly involved. The fact that Proctor could break her decision not to testify against Abigail prepares us for her reversal in Act Three when she caves in to accuse Proctor of witchcraft to save herself.

Major productions

On stage
The Crucible opened on 22 January 1953 at the Martin Beck Theater on Broadway. Despite its later success, the play's initial reception was mixed, though this might have been partly the result of its being perceived as a work critical of current politics. Although it won Tony and Donaldson Awards for Best Play, some critics were quick to condemn both play and playwright. The production only ran for 197 performances, 545 fewer than *Death of a Salesman*. After the tremendous success of *Death of a Salesman*, some critics felt let down, and saw *The Crucible* as less innovative and therefore a step backwards. Walter Kerr said it was too mechanical and overtly polemic. Eric Bentley notably attacked the play,

claiming that Miller's naive liberalism and depiction of
innocence reduced it to melodrama. Even Miller's staunch
ally at the *New York Times*, Brooks Atkinson, had
reservations, concerned that the play was 'more like a tract
than a drama about people'.

There were difficulties with the initial production.
Unwilling to work with Elia Kazan, because of the director's
friendly testimony before HUAC, Miller had to find
someone else to produce his play. Despite a reputation for
being difficult, Jed Harris took on the assignment. His
working relationship with Miller was strained from the start.
Harris disliked Miller's choice of Arthur Kennedy to play
Proctor, and demanded a series of rewrites in an
unsuccessful attempt to undermine the playwright's
confidence so that he might gain full control of the
production. His direction of the play was static; characters
made speeches to the audience rather than to each other
and Harris kept them frozen in tableaux while speaking
their lines. This approach made critics view the play as cold
and unemotional. After the initial reviews, Harris withdrew
from the production and left Miller to try to salvage the
show. Miller tightened the script and added a new scene at
the close of the second act between Proctor and Abigail,
recycled from an earlier draft of the play. Yet the New York
production never captured the play's momentum.

In 1958 the Martinique Theatre was built out of an old
hotel ballroom. The arena stage that resulted allowed for
The Crucible to be presented in the round, which instantly
made it more accessible. Henry Hewes felt it had 'more
emotional impact' than the original Broadway production,
and Lewis Funke admired its 'absorbing vitality', describing
it as 'provocative' and 'stimulating'. Atkinson changed his
mind about the play, praising its more vibrant staging,
fluent pacing and the way the characters were presented
with admirable modulation. Utilising moody lighting, Word
Baker kept a fast directorial pace by having his actors
change props. Miller wrote additional background
information inserted into the first act. Though rarely
included in performances since, these notes were read aloud

by an additional character, the Reader. Baker also placed a
strong focus on Proctor, played with simplicity and vigour
by Michael Higgins, making the role more clearly the play's
centre. After several extensions, the production ran for 653
performances, proving the play's theatrical strength.

The play's emotional plot was nowhere better suggested
than in Robert Ward's 1961 operatic version.
Commissioned by the Ford Foundation for the New York
City Opera, Ward was inspired by the 1958 Off-Broadway
show. Drawn by what he saw as Miller's stylised rhetoric
and a strong plot he felt was well-suited to the compression
of a libretto, Ward persuaded an initially reluctant Miller to
agree to this adaptation. Bernard Stambler's libretto cut a
third of Miller's text, but changed very little of the play's
essential nature. It eliminated Herrick and Hathorne, added
more girls and a prison guard, and compressed the time-
scale. Using a split-level set allowed individual singers to
play key scenes above the chorus of townspeople, and it
gave them greater prominence. The operatic format
heightened its theatrical intensity, and Frank Merling
suggested that 'the score adds something to the story: a non-
topical sense of the development of the greatness of the
human spirit'. John Rockwell would later call it 'one of the
most powerfully affecting of all America's operas,
capitalizing on the play's strength and adding a striking
musical subtext'. Winthrop Sargeant declared it a 'smash
hit' and a worthwhile occasion for 'thunderous and heartfelt
applause'. It won a Pulitzer Prize for music in 1962.

Ten years later the Repertory Theater of Lincoln Center
had a hit production, directed by John Berry. He was the
first to emphasise the play's sexual rivalry and suggest
sympathy for Abigail – perhaps a reflection of changing
mores – as well as revealing contemporary connections to
concerns about authority and truth during the Vietnam
War. Pamela Payton-Wright's Abigail was portrayed as
genuinely loving Proctor and highly aggrieved by his
rejection, while Robert Foxworth's Proctor, spoken with a
British North Country accent, became a representative of
the working class when he spoke against the pompous

magistrates and greedy landowners. Harold Clurman
praised the 'unity' of the production and Clive Barnes its
'moral force' and 'great dramatic impact'.

Staged by Jo Mielziner, who designed the original set for
Death of a Salesman, audiences saw a virtually empty stage on
which projections and light changes were used to indicate
the scene. The decision had been partly induced by the
Center's need for a frugal production; they could not afford
expensive sets and asked Mielziner to use existing lighting
from a previous production. Mary Henderson describes
Mielziner's stylised design as using only a few items of
furniture and props, which were made slightly overscale to
dwarf the characters and make them look like 'human
pawns in a larger tragic game'. Set against two sloping
planes that came to a point at the back, the concept allowed
for greater focus on the actors. Emphasising Miller's
references to light in the play, Mielziner lit Betty's bedroom
from the outside. At the close of Act Two the cast appeared
on the forestage singing a hymn, while an eerie light shone
from below to suggest the flames of hell this community had
unleashed. Act Three utilised a barred wooden partition
through which light could stream over the magistrate's desk
and oversized chair, as well as over the forestage where the
accused would stand. In the final act Mielziner placed a
large barred window high on the right wall to cast
additional shafts of light across the entire stage.

After numerous Off-Broadway and regional productions,
the play's fifth Broadway revival in 2002 emphasised the
relationship between the Proctors rather than that between
Proctor and Abigail and cast major stars – Liam Neeson
and Laura Linney – in these roles. Directed by Richard
Eyre, it won a Tony for Best Revival and several other
nominations. The stars dominated the show, but this offered
an interesting take on the Proctors' relationship. Neeson and
Linney portrayed a more evident sexual relationship than
usual, with Proctor purposefully stripping off his shirt to
wash himself in front of his wife, while she struggled to
control her emotional responses towards him. In this
production Angela Bettis's Abigail was decidedly unsexy,

played as a sullen teen. Though this made Proctor's adultery less credible, it focused the production on how a problematic marriage survives.

There have been just as many laudable British productions. The first, in 1954 at Bristol Old Vic, like the Broadway premiere, garnered mixed reviews and was considered melodramatic. But when Laurence Olivier directed Colin Blakely as Proctor at the Old Vic in 1965, the play, featuring strong ensemble acting, was well received by British critics. It raised the production above charges of melodrama. Though interested in the play's sexual themes and the relationship between Proctor and Abigail, Olivier deleted the additional scene between them in order to respect the rising dynamic of the play. Robert Brustein, who had originally disliked the play, felt that under Olivier it took 'on some of the proportions of a Shakespearian tragedy'. For Brustein, the English country accents of the cast gave the dialogue both vigour and authority.

In 1980 *The Crucible* was produced in the National Theatre's smaller theatre, the Cottesloe. Directed by Bill Bryden, with Mark McManus as Proctor, it garnered positive reviews and transferred to the Comedy Theatre in 1981. The National produced the play again, this time in its large Olivier Theatre, just ten years later, with Tom Wilkinson in the role of Proctor. This volatile production, directed by Howard Davies, received mixed reviews but had a generally positive response from large audiences. With fast pacing and strong acting, Davies tried to draw audiences into the group hysteria and make them feel the intensity of the domestic situation. In between the National productions, there was also a much lionised and fervent production at the Young Vic in 1985 directed by David Thacker, who would go on to direct the British premieres of several of Miller's later plays. Thacker paid close attention to individual characterisations and produced a finely detailed piece that Matt Wolf praised for 'bringing this drama's contemporary reverberations thrillingly, ringingly alive'.

Britain's 2006 revival at the Royal Shakespeare Company, on the main stage in Stratford, transferred to the

West End to win the Olivier Award for Best Revival. The director Dominic Cooke also saw Shakespearean dimensions in the play and its relevance to a post-9/11 society in which politicians exploited public fear to destroy civil liberties and create scapegoats. The *Guardian* said that Cooke brought out 'the play's political urgency' and praised Iain Glen's Proctor as 'a figure of Lawrentian power and sensuality' pitted against Elaine Cassidy's Abigail, who was 'not the usual diabolical nymphet, but a young girl whose sexual stirrings find no outlet in this community'. This allowed Abigail to be as much a victim as those put on trial, a reflection, no doubt, of increased feminist awareness.

Hildegard Bechtler's set design for this production was faithful to the period but extremely austere, in order to focus attention on the actors and reflect the simplicity of the Puritan world. The production began with a view of the woods, eerily lit, before the back wall closed to form Betty's sparse bedroom. The trees remained visible through a large rear window in order to emphasise the ever-threatening mysteries faced by the early settlers. The courtroom scene emulated Mielziner's 1972 design, shooting shafts of light through high-barred windows on to the opposing wall. At the play's close the wall again parted as the condemned were led out into the woods to be hanged. This gave the impression of a lynching rather than anything resembling a regulated judicial system. The *Daily Telegraph* described this interpretation as a 'shatteringly powerful production that never releases its grip for a moment'.

On film

In 1957 the first film of Miller's play was produced in France, with a screenplay by the writer and philosopher Jean-Paul Sartre. He depicted the play as a conflict between capitalists and heroic Marxists. Retitled *Les Sorcières de Salem*, or *The Witches of Salem*, Miller felt that the Marxist references Sartre included were too heavy-handed. Most critics agreed. Directed by Raymond Borderie and starring Yves Montand and Simone Signoret, the film met mixed reviews. Bosley

Crowther called it a 'persistently absorbing film' with 'outstanding performances', while Stanley Kauffmann noted that Sartre's emphasis on socialist political agitation distorted the drama. In *Time* magazine Isabel Quigly saw the film as both forbidding and insightful, but sadly an 'appalling politically pointed tale' that missed the mark by identifying 'the witch burners as colonial capitalists and the hero as a son of the suffering masses'.

There have been several television versions of the play, including two in 1959: the Canadian Broadcasting Corporation production with Leslie Nielsen and Diana Maddox, and another by Granada TV in England, with Sean Connery and Susannah York. Alex Segal directed a version for CBS in 1967 with George C. Scott, but Jack Gould felt it lacked tension and seemed 'cold and remote'. None of these versions was highly acclaimed, although they served to introduce the play to a large number of viewers. More successful was Louis Mark's 1982 production for BBC television, which portrayed Proctor as a 'damaged man' who rises against injustice.

The film version of *The Crucible* with which Miller was most closely involved – and for which he rewrote scenes, added others and streamlined the rhetoric – was made in 1996 for Twentieth-Century Fox. While fastidious attention was paid to making the setting and costumes authentic, a national controversy contemporary with the film's production was the sexual scandal of President Clinton; this version emphasises the play's accent on the hypocrisy of religious zealots and the dangers of sexual repression and the political chaos to which this can lead. Such emphasis took it away from its increasingly less-known 1950s roots, but in the eyes of many critics made it more accessible. Directed by Nicholas Hytner, it starred Winona Ryder, Joan Allen, and Daniel Day Lewis. The sexual aspects of the story are evident from the opening sequence, one in which we see a group of Salem girls make love charms with Tituba in order to catch husbands for themselves. Sex is on everyone's mind, but it is something that can only be discussed in the dark woods. Abigail is teased by her friends

for wanting Proctor, and Tituba objects to making a charm
to bind a married man. Abigail's wild response is to smear
her face with chicken blood and incite the girls into a
raucous and sensual dance. The sexual tension between
Proctor and Abigail is insistent from their first appearance
together and continues in each subsequent encounter.

As a teenager passionately and fatally in love with a
married man, the role of Abigail is presented with
sympathy. When she and Proctor first talk together, their
mutual attraction is evident. Proctor is clearly resisting
temptation and trying to calm the fire between them. When
Abigail kisses and gropes him, he lingers before turning
away. Their second meeting takes place earlier in the
timeline, before Elizabeth has even been charged, with
Proctor asking Abigail not to name his wife. This acts as a
goad for Abigail, the thwarted lover, to do just that. Before
she leaves town near the close, Abigail visits Proctor in his
chains and begs him to go with her, declaring 'I never
dreamed any of this for you. I wanted you, that is all.' He
refuses, saying they can only meet again in hell, where he
sees both heading as a consequence of their past adultery.
Yet Miller seems to want the audience to view the coupling
of Proctor and Abigail more sympathetically. Proctor is
depicted as a man caught between two passions, and his
dealings with Abigail have been something more than mere
casual sex.

Another major change is the addition of Judge Sewell,
who offers a voice of reason. He warns the others from the
start against the possibility of madness in their witnesses and
therefore becomes a counterpoint to Danforth's stern
insistence. Sewell wonders about the number of children
involved, recognises the land-grabbing truth behind
Putnam's accusations, and is uncertain about the
accusations from the very first hanging. However, Danforth
has a superior authority and dismisses his concerns, bullying
him into compliance. Danforth seems less the rule-bearer
than egoist; he thinks he knows best, demanding full control.
When Abigail, worried that Hale might be about to
interfere, accuses Hale's wife, Danforth refuses to listen,

insisting she is mistaken because a minister's wife is inviolable.

The film shows the Salemites celebrating as the first group is hanged, but their hysteria dies down as the presence of death begins to pall. We see them beginning to spurn Abigail, provoking her departure, and when the time comes to hang Proctor, alongside Rebecca and Martha, the townspeople are far less enthusiastic. Several call 'God bless you' to the gallows as they pass, and they stand watching silently, weeping in disbelief as the three are hanged. Rebecca begins to recite the Lord's Prayer and Martha and Proctor join in for the closing 'for ever and ever'. But no one says 'Amen' as the film cuts to a tight shot on the hanging rope. This ending underlines who the godless truly are and it is little wonder that no one who witnesses the executions can sign off on the central prayer of their faith. Significantly, in this trinity of death, Proctor is central, thus reinforcing his connection to a beleaguered Christ, one made earlier in the film by his crucifixion pose when he is first arrested. Richard A. Blake saw the film 'as an incisive examination of the human condition', and Edward Guthmann as 'at once stunningly cinematic and perfectly faithful to Miller's text'. Jay Carr praised the film, announcing the drama to be 'more electrifying than ever, boldly focusing as much on repressed sexuality as on political paranoia and conflagration'.

Further Reading

Works by Miller

Arthur Miller Plays, 6 vols (vol. 1: *All My Sons, Death of a Salesman, The Crucible, A Memory of Two Mondays, A View from the Bridge*; vol. 2: *The Misfits, After the Fall, Incident at Vichy, The Price, Creation of the World, Playing for Time*; vol. 3: *The American Clock, The Archbishop's Ceiling, Two-Way Mirror*; vol. 4: *The Golden Years, The Man Who Had All the Luck, I Can't Remember Anything, Clara*; vol. 5: *The Last Yankee, The Ride Down Mount Morgan, Almost Everybody Wins*; vol. 6: *Broken Glass, Mr Peters' Connections, Resurrection Blues, Finishing the Picture*), London: Methuen, 1988–2009

All My Sons, with commentary and notes by Toby Zinman. London: Methuen Drama, 2010

A View From the Bridge, with commentary and notes by Stephen Marino. London: Methuen Drama, 2010

Death of a Salesman, with commentary and notes by Enoch Brater. London: Methuen Drama, 2010

Echoes Down the Corridor, ed. Steven R. Centola. London: Methuen, 2001

'The Crucible' in History and Other Essays. London: Methuen, 2005

The Portable Arthur Miller, ed. Christopher Bigsby. Rev. ed. New York: Penguin, 2003

The Theatre Essays of Arthur Miller, ed. Robert A. Martin. London: Methuen, 1994

'Why I Wrote "*The Crucible*"'. *New Yorker* (21–8 October 1996): 158–60

Full-length studies of Miller

Abbotson, Susan C. W., *Critical Companion to Arthur Miller*. New York: Facts on File, 2008

—, *Student Companion to Arthur Miller*. Westport, CT: Greenwood Press, 2000

Bigsby, Christopher, *Arthur Miller: A Critical Study*. Cambridge: Cambridge University Press, 2005

—, *Arthur Miller: The Definitive Biography*. London: Weidenfeld & Nicolson, 2008

—, ed. *The Cambridge Companion to Arthur Miller*. Cambridge: Cambridge University Press, 1997

Brater, Enoch, *Arthur Miller: A Playwright's Life and Work*. London: Thames and Hudson, 2005

—, ed. *Arthur Miller's America: Theater and Culture in a Time of Change*. Ann Arbor, MI: University of Michigan Press, 2005

—, ed. *Arthur Miller's Global Theater*. Ann Arbor , MI: University of Michigan Press, 2007

Carson, Neil, *Arthur Miller*. 2nd. edn,. London: Macmillan, 2008

Centola, Steven, ed. *The Achievement of Arthur Miller: New Essays*. Dallas, TX: Contemporary Research, 1995

Gottfried, Martin, *Arthur Miller: His Life and Work*. New York: Da Capo, 2003

Marino, Stephen, *A Language Study of Arthur Miller's Plays: The Poetic in the Colloquial*. New York: Mellen, 2002

Martin, Robert A., ed. *Arthur Miller: New Perspectives*. Englewood Cliffs, N J: Prentice-Hall, 1982

Mason, Jeffrey, *Stone Tower: The Political Theater of Arthur Miller*. Ann Arbor, MI: University of Michigan Press, 2008

Otten, Terry, *The Temptation of Innocence in the Dramas of Arthur Miller*. Columbia, MO: University of Missouri Press, 2002

Savran, David, *Communists, Cowboys, and Queers: The Politics of Masculinity in the Work of Arthur Miller and Tennessee Williams*. Minneapolis, MN: University of Minneapolis Press, 1992

Schlueter, June, and James K. Flanagan, *Arthur Miller*. New York: Ungar, 1987

Welland, Dennis, *Miller: The Playwright*. 3rd edn. New York: Methuen, 1985

Studies of *The Crucible*

Alter, Iska, 'Betrayal and Blessedness: Explorations of Feminine Power in *The Crucible, A View from the Bridge*, and *After the Fall'*. *Feminist Rereadings of Modern American Drama*, ed. June Schlueter, Rutherford, NJ: Farleigh Dickinson University Press, 1989

Ardolino, Frank, 'Babylonian Confusion and Biblical Inversion in Miller's *The Crucible*'. *Journal of Evolutionary Psychology* 24.1–2 (March 2003): 64–72

Booth, David, 'Dubious American Ideal: Gender and Historical Knowledge in *The Crucible*'. *Soundings: An Interdisciplinary Journal* 84.1–2 (Spring–Summer 2001): 31–49

Caruso, Cristina C., "One Finds What One Seeks': Arthur Miller's *The Crucible* as a Regeneration of the American Myth of Violence'. *Journal of American Drama and Theatre* 7. 3 (Fall 1995): 30–42

DelFattore, Joan, 'Fueling the Fire of Hell: A Reply to Censors of *The Crucible*'. *Censored Books: Critical Viewpoints*, eds Nicholas Karolides, Lee Burress, and John M. Kean, Metuchen, NJ: Scarecrow, 1993: 201–8

Ferres, John H., ed. *Twentieth-Century Interpretations of 'The Crucible'*. Englewood Cliffs, NJ: Prentice-Hall, 1972

Hendrickson, Gary P., 'The Last Analogy: Arthur Miller's Witches and America's Domestic Communists'. *Midwest Quarterly* 33.4 (1992): 447–56

Lowe, Valerie, "'Unsafe Convictions": "Unhappy" Confessions in *The Crucible*'. *Language and Literature* 3.3 (1994): 175–95

Marino, Stephen, 'Arthur Miller's "Weight of Truth"'. *Modern Drama* 38.4 (Winter 1995): 488–95

Martin, Robert A., 'Arthur Miller's *The Crucible*: Background and Sources'. *Modern Drama* 20 (1977): 279–2

Martine, James J., *'The Crucible': Politics, Property, and Pretence*. New York: Twayne, 1993

Partridge, C. J., *The Crucible* Oxford: Blackwell, 1971

Pearson, Michelle, 'John Proctor and the Crucible of Individuation in Arthur Miller's *The Crucible*'. *Studies in American Drama* 6.1 (1991): 15–27

Schissel, Wendy, 'Re(dis)covering the Witches in Arthur Miller's *The Crucible*: A Feminist Reading'. *Modern Drama* 37.3 (1994): 461–73

Strout, Cushing, 'Analogical History: *The Crucible*'. *The Veracious Imagination*. Middletown, CT: Wesleyan University Press, 1981: 139–56

Valente, Joseph, 'Rehearsing the Witch Trials: Gender Injustice in *The Crucible*'. *New Formations* 32 (Autumn–Winter 1997): 120–34

The Crucible

A Play in Four Acts

A Note on the Historical Accuracy of this Play

This play is not history in the sense in which the word is used by the academic historian. Dramatic purposes have sometimes required many characters to be fused into one; the number of girls involved in the 'crying-out' has been reduced; Abigail's age has been raised; while there were several judges of almost equal authority, I have symbolized them all in Hathorne and Danforth. However, I believe that the reader will discover here the essential nature of one of the strangest and most awful chapters in human history. The fate of each character is exactly that of his historical model, and there is no one in the drama who did not play a similar – and in some cases exactly the same – role in history.

As for the characters of the persons, little is known about most of them excepting what may be surmised from a few letters, the trial record, certain broadsides written at the time, and references to their conduct in sources of varying reliability. They may therefore be taken as creations of my own, drawn to the best of my ability in conformity with their known behavior, except as indicated in the commentary I have written for this text.

Characters

Reverend Parris
Betty Parris
Tituba
Abigail Williams
Susanna Walcott
Mrs Ann Putnam
Thomas Putnam
Mercy Lewis
Mary Warren
John Proctor
Rebecca Nurse
Giles Corey
Reverend John Hale
Elizabeth Proctor
Francis Nurse
Ezekiel Cheever
Marshal Herrick
Judge Hathorne
Deputy Governor Danforth
Sarah Good
Hopkins

Act One
(An Overture)

A small upper bedroom in the home of **Reverend Samuel Parris**, *Salem, Massachusetts, in the spring of the year 1692.*

There is a narrow window at the left. Through its leaded panes the morning sunlight streams. A candle still burns near the bed, which is at the right. A chest, a chair, and a small table are the other furnishings. At the back a door opens on the landing of the stairway to the ground floor. The room gives off an air of clean spareness. The roof rafters are exposed, and the wood colors are raw and unmellowed.

As the curtain rises, **Reverend Parris** *is discovered kneeling beside the bed, evidently in prayer. His daughter,* **Betty Parris**, *aged ten, is lying on the bed, inert.*

At the time of these events Parris was in his middle forties. In history he cut a villainous path, and there is very little good to be said for him. He believed he was being persecuted wherever he went, despite his best efforts to win people and God to his side. In meeting, he felt insulted if someone rose to shut the door without first asking his permission. He was a widower with no interest in children, or talent with them. He regarded them as young adults, and until this strange crisis he, like the rest of Salem, never conceived that the children were anything but thankful for being permitted to walk straight, eyes slightly lowered, arms at the sides, and mouths shut until bidden to speak.

His house stood in the 'town' – but we today would hardly call it a village. The meeting house was nearby, and from this point outward – toward the bay or inland – there were a few small-windowed, dark houses snuggling against the raw Massachusetts winter. Salem had been established hardly forty years before. To the European world the whole province was a barbaric frontier inhabited by a sect of fanatics who, nevertheless, were shipping out products of slowly increasing quantity and value.

No one can really know what their lives were like. They had no novelists – and would not have permitted anyone to read a novel if one were handy. Their creed forbade anything resembling a theater or 'vain enjoyment'. They did not celebrate Christmas, and a holiday from work meant only that they must concentrate even more upon prayer.

Which is not to say that nothing broke into this strict and somber way of life. When a new farmhouse was built, friends assembled to 'raise the roof', and there would be special foods cooked and probably some potent cider passed around. There was a good supply of ne'er-do-wells in Salem, who dallied at the shovelboard in Bridget Bishop's tavern. Probably more than the creed, hard work kept the morals of the place from spoiling, for the people were forced to fight the land like heroes for every grain of corn, and no man had very much time for fooling around.

That there were some jokers, however, is indicated by the practice of appointing a two-man patrol whose duty was to 'walk forth in the time of God's worship to take notice of such as either lye about the meeting house, without attending to the word and ordinances, or that lye at home or in the fields without giving good account thereof, and to take the names of such persons, and to present them to the magistrates, whereby they may be accordingly proceeded against'. This predilection for minding other people's business was time-honored among the people of Salem, and it undoubtedly created many of the suspicions which were to feed the coming madness. It was also, in my opinion, one of the things that a John Proctor would rebel against, for the time of the armed camp had almost passed, and since the country was reasonably – although not wholly – safe, the old disciplines were beginning to rankle. But, as in all such matters, the issue was not clear-cut, for danger was still a possibility, and in unity still lay the best promise of safety.

The edge of the wilderness was close by. The American continent stretched endlessly west, and it was full of mystery for them. It stood, dark and threatening, over their shoulders night and day, for out of it Indian tribes marauded from time to time, and Reverend Parris had parishioners who had lost relatives to these heathen.

The parochial snobbery of these people was partly responsible for their failure to convert the Indians. Probably they also preferred to take land from heathens rather than from fellow Christians. At any rate, very few Indians were converted, and the Salem folk believed that the virgin forest was the Devil's last preserve, his home base and the citadel of his final stand. To the best of their knowledge the American forest was the last place on earth that was not paying homage to God.

For these reasons, among others, they carried about an air of innate resistance, even of persecution. Their fathers had, of course, been persecuted in England. So now they and their church found it necessary to deny any other sect its freedom, lest their New Jerusalem be defiled and corrupted by wrong ways and deceitful ideas.

They believed, in short, that they held in their steady hands the candle that would light the world. We have inherited this belief, and it has helped and hurt us. It helped them with the discipline it gave them. They were a dedicated folk, by and large, and they had to be to survive the life they had chosen or been born into in this country.

The proof of their belief's value to them may be taken from the opposite character of the first Jamestown settlement, farther south, in Virginia. The Englishmen who landed there were motivated mainly by a hunt for profit. They had thought to pick off the wealth of the new country and then return rich to England. They were a band of individualists, and a much more ingratiating group than the Massachusetts men. But Virginia destroyed them. Massachusetts tried to kill off the Puritans, but they combined; they set up a communal society which, in the beginning, was little more than an armed camp with an autocratic and very devoted leadership. It was, however, an autocracy by consent, for they were united from top to bottom by a commonly held ideology whose perpetuation was the reason and justification for all their sufferings. So their self-denial, their purposefulness, their suspicion of all vain pursuits, their hard-handed justice, were altogether perfect instruments for the conquest of this space so antagonistic to man.

But the people of Salem in 1692 were not quite the dedicated folk that arrived on the *Mayflower.* A vast differentiation had taken place, and in their own time a revolution had unseated the royal government and substituted a junta which was at this moment in power. The times, to their eyes, must have been out of joint, and to the common folk must have seemed as insoluble and complicated as do ours today. It is not hard to see how easily many could have been led to believe that the time of confusion had been brought upon them by deep and darkling forces. No hint of such speculation appears on the court record, but social disorder in any age breeds such mystical suspicions, and when, as in Salem, wonders are brought forth from below the social surface, it is too much to expect people to hold back very long from laying on the victims with all the force of their frustrations.

The Salem tragedy, which is about to begin in these pages, developed from a paradox. It is a paradox in whose grip we still live, and there is no prospect yet that we will discover its resolution. Simply, it was this: for good purposes, even high purposes, the people of Salem developed a theocracy, a combine of state and religious power whose function was to keep the community together, and to prevent any kind of disunity that might open it to destruction by material or ideological enemies. It was forged for a necessary purpose and accomplished that purpose. But all organization is and must be grounded on the idea of exclusion and prohibition, just as two objects cannot occupy the same space. Evidently the time came in New England when the repressions of order were heavier than seemed warranted by the dangers against which the order was organized. The witch-hunt was a perverse manifestation of the panic which set in among all classes when the balance began to turn toward greater individual freedom.

When one rises above the individual villainy displayed, one can only pity them all, just as we shall be pitied someday. It is still impossible for man to organize his social life without repressions, and the balance has yet to be struck between order and freedom.

The witch-hunt was not, however, a mere repression. It was also, and as importantly, a long overdue opportunity for everyone so inclined to express publicly his guilt and sins, under the cover of accusations against the victims. It suddenly became possible – and patriotic and holy – for a man to say that Martha

Corey had come into his bedroom at night, and that, while his wife was sleeping at his side, Martha laid herself down on his chest and 'nearly suffocated him'. Of course it was her spirit only, but his satisfaction at confessing himself was no lighter than if it had been Martha herself. One could not ordinarily speak such things in public.

Long-held hatreds of neighbors could now be openly expressed, and vengeance taken, despite the Bible's charitable injunctions. Land-lust which had been expressed before by constant bickering over boundaries and deeds, could now be elevated to the arena of morality; one could cry witch against one's neighbor and feel perfectly justified in the bargain. Old scores could be settled on a plane of heavenly combat between Lucifer and the Lord; suspicions and the envy of the miserable toward the happy could and did burst out in the general revenge.

Reverend Parris *is praying now, and, though we cannot hear his words, a sense of his confusion hangs about him. He mumbles, then seems about to weep, then he weeps, then prays again; but his daughter does not stir on the bed.*

The door opens, and his Negro slave enters. **Tituba** *is in her forties.* **Parris** *brought her with him from Barbados, where he spent some years as a merchant before entering the ministry. She enters as one does who can no longer bear to be barred from the sight of her beloved, but she is also very frightened because her slave sense has warned her that, as always, trouble in this house eventually lands on her back.*

Tituba (*already taking a step backward*)   My Betty be hearty soon?

Parris   Out of here!

Tituba (*backing to the door*)   My Betty not goin' die . . .

Parris (*scrambling to his feet in a fury*)   Out of my sight! (*She is gone.*) Out of my – (*He is overcome with sobs. He clamps his teeth against them and closes the door and leans against it, exhausted.*) Oh, my God! God help me! (*Quaking with fear, mumbling to himself through his sobs, he goes to the bed and gently takes* **Betty**'s *hand.*)

Betty. Child. Dear child. Will you wake, will you open up your eyes! Betty, little one . . .

He is bending to kneel again when his niece, **Abigail Williams**, *seventeen, enters – a strikingly beautiful girl, an orphan, with an endless capacity for dissembling. Now she is all worry and apprehension and propriety.*

Abigail   Uncle? (*He looks to her.*) Susanna Walcott's here from Doctor Griggs.

Parris   Oh? Let her come, let her come.

Abigail (*leaning out the door to call to* **Susanna**, *who is down the hall a few steps*)   Come in, Susanna.

Susanna Walcott, *a little younger than* **Abigail**, *a nervous, hurried girl, enters.*

Parris (*eagerly*)   What does the doctor say, child?

Susanna (*craning around* **Parris** *to get a look at* **Betty**)   He bid me come and tell you, reverend sir, that he cannot discover no medicine for it in his books.

Parris   Then he must search on.

Susanna   Aye, sir, he have been searchin' his books since he left you, sir. But he bid me tell you, that you might look to unnatural things for the cause of it.

Parris (*his eyes going wide*)   No – no. There be no unnatural cause here. Tell him I have sent for Reverend Hale of Beverly, and Mr Hale will surely confirm that. Let him look to medicine and put out all thought of unnatural causes here. There be none.

Susanna   Aye, sir. He bid me tell you. (*She turns to go.*)

Abigail   Speak nothin' of it in the village, Susanna.

Parris   Go directly home and speak nothing of unnatural causes.

Susanna   Aye, sir. I pray for her. (*She goes out.*)

Abigail   Uncle, the rumor of witchcraft is all about; I think you'd best go down and deny it yourself. The parlor's packed with people, sir. I'll sit with her.

Parris (*pressed, turns on her*)   And what shall I say to them? That my daughter and my niece I discovered dancing like heathen in the forest?

Abigail   Uncle, we did dance; let you tell them I confessed it and I'll be whipped if I must be. But they're speakin' of witchcraft. Betty's not witched.

Parris   Abigail, I cannot go before the congregation when I know you have not opened with me. What did you do with her in the forest?

Abigail   We did dance, uncle, and when you leaped out of the bush so suddenly, Betty was frightened and then she fainted. And there's the whole of it.

Parris   Child. Sit you down.

Abigail (*quavering, as she sits*)   I would never hurt Betty. I love her dearly.

Parris   Now look you, child, your punishment will come in its time. But if you trafficked with spirits in the forest, I must know it now, for surely my enemies will, and they will ruin me with it.

Abigail   But we never conjured spirits.

Parris   Then why can she not move herself since midnight? This child is desperate! (**Abigail** *lowers her eyes.*) It must come out, my enemies will bring it out. Let me know what you done there. Abigail, do you understand that I have many enemies?

Abigail   I have heard of it, uncle.

Parris   There is a faction that is sworn to drive me from my pulpit. Do you understand that?

Abigail   I think so, sir.

Parris   Now then, in the midst of such disruption, my own household is discovered to be the very center of some obscene practice. Abominations are done in the forest –

Abigail   It were sport, uncle!

Parris (*pointing at* **Betty**)   You call this sport? (*She lowers her eyes. He pleads.*) Abigail, if you know something that may help the doctor, for God's sake tell it to me. (*She is silent.*) I saw Tituba waving her arms over the fire when I came on you. Why was she doing that? And I heard a screeching and gibberish coming from her mouth. She were swaying like a dumb beast over that fire!

Abigail   She always sings her Barbados songs, and we dance.

Parris   I cannot blink what I saw, Abigail, for my enemies will not blink it. I saw a dress lying on the grass.

Abigail (*innocently*)   A dress?

Parris (*it is very hard to say*)   Aye, a dress. And I thought I saw – someone naked running through the trees!

Abigail (*in terror*)   No one was naked! You mistake yourself, uncle!

Parris (*with anger*)   I saw it! (*He moves from her. Then, resolved.*) Now tell me true, Abigail. And I pray you feel the weight of truth upon you, for now my ministry's at stake, my ministry and perhaps your cousin's life. Whatever abomination you have done, give me all of it now, for I dare not be taken unaware when I go before them down there.

Abigail   There is nothin' more. I swear it, uncle.

Parris (*studies her, then nods, half convinced*)   Abigail, I have fought here three long years to bend these stiff-necked people to me, and now, just now when some good respect is rising for me in the parish, you compromise my very character. I have given you a home, child, I have put clothes upon your back – now give me upright answer. Your name in the town – it is entirely white, is it not?

Abigail (*with an edge of resentment*)   Why, I am sure it is, sir. There be no blush about my name.

Parris (*to the point*)   Abigail, is there any other cause than you have told me, for your being discharged from Goody Proctor's service? I have heard it said, and I tell you as I heard it, that she comes so rarely to the church this year for she will not sit so close to something soiled. What signified that remark?

Abigail   She hates me, uncle, she must, for I would not be her slave. It's a bitter woman, a lying, cold, sniveling woman, and I will not work for such a woman!

Parris   She may be. And yet it has troubled me that you are now seven month out of their house, and in all this time no other family has ever called for your service.

Abigail   They want slaves, not such as I. Let them send to Barbados for that. I will not black my face for any of them! (*With ill-concealed resentment at him.*) Do you begrudge my bed, uncle?

Parris   No – no.

Abigail (*in a temper*)   My name is good in the village! I will not have it said my name is soiled! Goody Proctor is a gossiping liar!

Enter **Mrs Ann Putnam**. *She is a twisted soul of forty-five, a death-ridden woman, haunted by dreams.*

Parris (*as soon as the door begins to open*)   No, I cannot have anyone. (*He sees her, and a certain deference springs into him, although his worry remains.*) Why, Goody Putnam, come in.

Mrs Putnam (*full of breath, shiny-eyed*)   It is a marvel. It is surely a stroke of hell upon you.

Parris   No, Goody Putnam, it is –

Mrs Putnam (*glancing at* **Betty**)   How high did she fly, how high?

Parris   No, no, she never flew –

Mrs Putnam (*very pleased with it*)   Why, it's sure she did. Mr Collins saw her goin' over Ingersoll's barn, and come down light as bird, he says!

Parris   Now, look you, Goody Putnam, she never – (*Enter* **Thomas Putnam**, *a well-to-do hard-handed landowner, near fifty.*) Oh, good morning, Mr Putnam.

Putnam   It is a providence the thing is out now! It is a providence. (*He goes directly to the bed.*)

Parris   What's out, sir, what's – ?

Mrs Putnam *goes to the bed.*

Putnam (*looking down at* **Betty**)   Why, *her* eyes is closed! Look you, Ann.

Mrs Putnam   Why, that's strange. (*To* **Parris**.) Ours is open.

Parris (*shocked*)   Your Ruth is sick?

Mrs Putnam (*with vicious certainty*)   I'd not call it sick; the Devil's touch is heavier than sick. It's death, y'know, it's death drivin' into them, forked and hoofed.

Parris   Oh, pray not! Why, how does Ruth ail?

Mrs Putnam   She ails as she must – she never waked this morning, but her eyes open and she walks, and hears naught, sees naught, and cannot eat. Her soul is taken, surely.

Parris *is struck.*

Putnam (*as though for further details*)   They say you've sent for Reverend Hale of Beverly?

Parris (*with dwindling conviction now*)   A precaution only. He has much experience in all demonic arts, and –

Mrs Putnam   He has indeed; and found a witch in Beverly last year, and let you remember that.

Parris   Now, Goody Ann, they only thought that were a witch, and I am certain there be no element of witchcraft here.

Putnam   No witchcraft! Now look you, Mr Parris –

Parris   Thomas, Thomas, I pray you, leap not to witchcraft.
I know that you – you least of all, Thomas, would ever wish so
disastrous a charge laid upon me. We cannot leap to witchcraft.
They will howl me out of Salem for such corruption in my
house.

A word about Thomas Putnam. He was a man with many grievances, at least one of which appears justified. Some time before,
his wife's brother-in-law, James Bayley, had been turned down
as minister of Salem. Bayley had all the qualifications, and a
two-thirds vote into the bargain, but a faction stopped his acceptance, for reasons that are not clear.

Thomas Putnam was the eldest son of the richest man in the
village. He had fought the Indians at Narragansett, and was
deeply interested in parish affairs. He undoubtedly felt it poor
payment that the village should so blatantly disregard his candi-
date for one of its more important offices, especially since he regarded himself as the intellectual superior of most of the people
around him.

His vindictive nature was demonstrated long before the witchcraft began. Another former Salem minister, George Burroughs,
had had to borrow money to pay for his wife's funeral, and,
since the parish was remiss in his salary, he was soon bankrupt.
Thomas and his brother John had Burroughs jailed for debts
the man did not owe. The incident is important only in that
Burroughs succeeded in becoming minister where Bayley,
Thomas Putnam's brother-in-law, had been rejected; the motif
of resentment is clear here. Thomas Putnam felt that his own
name and the honor of his family had been smirched by the
village, and he meant to right matters however he could.

Another reason to believe him a deeply embittered man was
his attempt to break his father's will, which left a disproportion-
ate amount to a stepbrother. As with every other public cause in
which he tried to force his way, he failed in this.

So it is not surprising to find that so many accusations against
people are in the handwriting of Thomas Putnam, or that his

name is so often found as a witness corroborating the super-
natural testimony, or that his daughter led the crying-out at the
most opportune junctures of the trials, especially when – But
we'll speak of that when we come to it.

Putnam (*at the moment he is intent upon getting* **Parris***, for whom he
has only contempt, to move toward the abyss*)   Mr Parris, I have taken
your part in all contention here, and I would continue; but I
cannot if you hold back in this. There are hurtful, vengeful spirits
layin' hands on these children.

Parris   But, Thomas, you cannot –

Putnam   Ann! Tell Mr Parris what you have done.

Mrs Putnam   Reverend Parris, I have laid seven babies
unbaptized in the earth. Believe me, sir, you never saw more
hearty babies born. And yet, each would wither in my arms
the very night of their birth. I have spoke nothin', but my
heart has clamored intimations. And now, this year, my Ruth,
my only – I see her turning strange. A secret child she has
become this year, and shrivels like a sucking mouth were pullin'
on her life too. And so I thought to send her to your Tituba –

Parris   To Tituba! What may Tituba – ?

Mrs Putnam   Tituba knows how to speak to the dead, Mr
Parris.

Parris   Goody Ann, it is a formidable sin to conjure up the
dead!

Mrs Putnam   I take it on my soul, but who else may surely
tell us what person murdered my babies?

Parris (*horrified*)   Woman!

Mrs Putnam   They were murdered, Mr Parris! And mark
this proof! Mark it! Last night my Ruth were ever so close to
their little spirits; I know it, sir. For how else is she struck dumb
now except some power of darkness would stop her mouth?
It is a marvelous sign, Mr Parris!

Putnam   Don't you understand it, sir? There is a murdering witch among us, bound to keep herself in the dark. (**Parris** *turns to* **Betty**, *a frantic terror rising in him.*) Let your enemies make of it what they will, you cannot blink it more.

Parris (*to* **Abigail**)   Then you were conjuring spirits last night.

Abigail (*whispering*)   Not I, sir – Tituba and Ruth.

Parris (*turns now, with new fear, and goes to* **Betty**, *looks down at her, and then, gazing off*)   Oh, Abigail, what proper payment for my charity! Now I am undone.

Putnam   You are not undone! Let you take hold here. Wait for no one to charge you – declare it yourself. You have discovered witchcraft –

Parris   In my house? In my house, Thomas? They will topple me with this! They will make of it a –

Enter **Mercy Lewis**, *the* **Putnams**' *servant, a fat, sly, merciless girl of eighteen.*

Mercy   Your pardons. I only thought to see how Betty is.

Putnam   Why aren't you home? Who's with Ruth?

Mercy   Her grandma come. She's improved a little, I think – she give a powerful sneeze before.

Mrs Putnam   Ah, there's a sign of life!

Mercy   I'd fear no more, Goody Putnam. It were a grand sneeze; another like it will shake her wits together, I'm sure. (*She goes to the bed to look.*)

Parris   Will you leave me now, Thomas? I would pray a while alone.

Abigail   Uncle, you've prayed since midnight. Why do you not go down and –

Parris   No – no. (*To* **Putnam**.) I have no answer for that crowd. I'll wait till Mr Hale arrives. (*To get* **Mrs Putnam** *to leave.*) If you will, Goody Ann . . .

Putnam   Now look you, sir. Let you strike out against the Devil, and the village will bless you for it! Come down, speak to them, pray with them. They're thirsting for your word, Mister! Surely you'll pray with them.

Parris (*swayed*)   I'll lead them in a psalm, but let you say nothing of witchcraft yet. I will not discuss it. The cause is yet unknown. I have had enough contention since I came; I want no more.

Mrs Putnam   Mercy, you go home to Ruth, d'y'hear?

Mercy   Aye, mum.

Mrs Putnam *goes out.*

Parris (*to* **Abigail**)   If she starts for the window, cry for me at once.

Abigail   I will, uncle.

Parris (*to* **Putnam**)   There is a terrible power in her arms today. (*He goes out with* **Putnam**.)

Abigail (*with hushed trepidation*)   How is Ruth sick?

Mercy   It's weirdish, I know not – she seems to walk like a dead one since last night.

Abigail (*turns at once and goes to* **Betty**, *and now, with fear in her voice*)   Betty? (**Betty** *doesn't move. She shakes her.*) Now stop this! Betty! Sit up now!

Betty *doesn't stir.* **Mercy** *comes over.*

Mercy   Have you tried beatin' her? I gave Ruth a good one and it waked her for a minute. Here, let me have her.

Abigail (*holding* **Mercy** *back*)   No, he'll be comin' up. Listen, now; if they be questioning us, tell them we danced – I told him as much already.

Mercy   Aye. And what more?

Abigail   He knows Tituba conjured Ruth's sisters to come out of the grave.

Mercy   And what more?

Abigail   He saw you naked.

Mercy (*clapping her hands together with a frightened laugh*)   Oh, Jesus!

Enter **Mary Warren**, *breathless. She is seventeen, a subservient, naive, lonely girl.*

Mary Warren   What'll we do? The village is out! I just come from the farm; the whole country's talkin' witchcraft! They'll be callin' us witches, Abby!

Mercy (*pointing and looking at* **Mary Warren**)   She means to tell, I know it.

Mary Warren   Abby, we've got to tell. Witchery's a hangin' error, a hangin' like they done in Boston two year ago! We must tell the truth, Abby! You'll only be whipped for dancin', and the other things!

Abigail   Oh, *we'll* be whipped!

Mary Warren   I never done none of it, Abby. I only looked!

Mercy (*moving menacingly toward* **Mary**)   Oh, you're a great one for lookin', aren't you, Mary Warren? What a grand peeping courage you have!

Betty, *on the bed, whimpers.* **Abigail** *turns to her at once.*

Abigail   Betty? (*She goes to* **Betty**.) Now, Betty, dear, wake up now. It's Abigail. (*She sits* **Betty** *up and furiously shakes her.*) I'll beat you, Betty! (**Betty** *whimpers.*) My, you seem improving. I talked to your papa and I told him everything. So there's nothing to –

Betty (*darts off the bed frightened of* **Abigail**, *and flattens herself against the wall*)   I want my mama!

Abigail (*with alarm as she cautiously approaches* **Betty**)   What ails you, Betty? Your mama's dead and buried.

Betty   I'll fly to Mama. Let me fly! (*She raises her arms as though to fly, and streaks for the window, gets one leg out.*)

Abigail (*pulling her away from the window*)   I told him everything; he knows now, he knows everything we –

Betty   You drank blood, Abby! You didn't tell him that!

Abigail   Betty, you never say that again! You will never –

Betty   You did, you did! You drank a charm to kill John Proctor's wife! You drank a charm to kill Goody Proctor!

Abigail (*smashes her across the face*)   Shut it! Now shut it!

Betty (*collapsing on the bed*)   Mama, Mama! (*She dissolves into sobs.*)

Abigail   Now look you. All of you. We danced. And Tituba conjured Ruth Putnam's dead sisters. And that is all. And mark this. Let either of you breathe a word, or the edge of a word, about the other things, I will come to you in the black of some terrible night and I will bring a pointy reckoning that will shudder you. And you know I can do it; I saw Indians smash my dear parents' heads on the pillow next to mine, and I have seen some reddish work done at night, and I can make you wish you had never seen the sun go down! (*She goes to* **Betty** *and roughly sits her up.*) Now, you – sit up and stop this!

But **Betty** *collapses in her hands and lies inert on the bed.*

Mary Warren (*with hysterical fright*)   What's got her? (**Abigail** *stares in fright at* **Betty**.) Abby, she's going to die! It's a sin to conjure and we –

Abigail (*starting for* **Mary**)   I say shut it, Mary Warren!

Enter **John Proctor**. *On seeing him,* **Mary Warren** *leaps in fright.*

Proctor was a farmer in his middle thirties. He need not have been a partisan of any faction in the town, but there is evidence to suggest that he had a sharp and biting way with hypocrites. He was the kind of man – powerful of body, even-tempered, and not easily led – who cannot refuse support to partisans without drawing their deepest resentment. In Proctor's presence a fool felt his foolishness instantly – and a Proctor is always marked for calumny therefore.

But as we shall see, the steady manner he displays does not spring from an untroubled soul. He is a sinner, a sinner not only against the moral fashion of the time, but against his own vision of decent conduct. These people had no ritual for the washing away of sins. It is another trait we inherited from them, and it has helped to discipline us as well as to breed hypocrisy among us. Proctor, respected and even feared in Salem, has come to regard himself as a kind of fraud. But no hint of this has yet appeared on the surface, and as he enters from the crowded parlor below it is a man in his prime we see, with a quiet confidence and an unexpressed, hidden force. Mary Warren, his servant, can barely speak for embarrassment and fear.

Mary Warren   Oh! I'm just going home, Mr Proctor.

Proctor   Be you foolish, Mary Warren? Be you deaf? I forbid you leave the house, did I not? Why shall I pay you? I am looking for you more often than my cows!

Mary Warren   I only come to see the great doings in the world.

Proctor   I'll show you a great doin' on your arse one of these days. Now get you home; my wife is waitin' with your work! (*Trying to retain a shred of dignity, she goes slowly out.*)

Mercy Lewis (*both afraid of him and strangely titillated*)   I'd best be off. I have my Ruth to watch. Good morning, Mr Proctor.

Mercy *sidles out. Since* **Proctor**'*s entrance,* **Abigail** *has stood as though on tiptoe, absorbing his presence, wide-eyed. He glances at her, then goes to* **Betty** *on the bed.*

Abigail   Gah! I'd almost forgot how strong you are, John Proctor!

Proctor (*looking at* **Abigail** *now, the faintest suggestion of a knowing smile on his face*)   What's this mischief here?

Abigail (*with a nervous laugh*)   Oh, she's only gone silly somehow.

Proctor   The road past my house is a pilgrimage to Salem all morning. The town's mumbling witchcraft.

Abigail   Oh, posh! (*Winningly she comes a little closer, with a confidential, wicked air.*) We were dancin' in the woods last night, and my uncle leaped in on us. She took fright, is all.

Proctor (*his smile widening*)   Ah, you're wicked yet, aren't y'! (*A trill of expectant laughter escapes her, and she dares come closer, feverishly looking into his eyes.*) You'll be clapped in the stocks before you're twenty.

He takes a step to go, and she springs into his path.

Abigail   Give me a word, John. A soft word. (*Her concentrated desire destroys his smile.*)

Proctor   No, no, Abby. That's done with.

Abigail (*tauntingly*)   You come five mile to see a silly girl fly? I know you better.

Proctor (*setting her firmly out of his path*)   I come to see what mischief your uncle's brewin' now. (*With final emphasis.*) Put it out of mind, Abby.

Abigail (*grasping his hand before he can release her*)   John – I am waitin' for you every night.

Proctor   Abby, I never give you hope to wait for me.

Abigail (*now beginning to anger – she can't believe it*)   I have something better than hope, I think!

Proctor   Abby, you'll put it out of mind. I'll not be comin' for you more.

Abigail   You're surely sportin' with me.

Proctor   You know me better.

Abigail   I know how you clutched my back behind your house and sweated like a stallion whenever I come near! Or did I dream that? It's she put me out, you cannot pretend it were you. I saw your face when she put me out, and you loved me then and you do now!

Proctor   Abby, that's a wild thing to say –

Abigail   A wild thing may say wild things. But not so wild, I think. I have seen you since she put me out; I have seen you nights.

Proctor   I have hardly stepped off my farm this sevenmonth.

Abigail   I have a sense for heat, John, and yours has drawn me to my window, and I have seen you looking up, burning in your loneliness. Do you tell me you've never looked up at my window?

Proctor   I may have looked up.

Abigail (*now softening*)   And you must. You are no wintry man. I know you, John. I *know* you. (*She is weeping.*) I cannot sleep for dreamin'; I cannot dream but I wake and walk about the house as though I'd find you comin' through some door. (*She clutches him desperately.*)

Proctor (*gently pressing her from him, with great sympathy but firmly*) Child –

Abigail (*with a flash of anger*)   How do you call me child!

Proctor   Abby, I may think of you softly from time to time. But I will cut off my hand before I'll ever reach for you again. Wipe it out of mind. We never touched, Abby.

Abigail   Aye – but we did.

Proctor   Aye, but we did not.

Abigail (*with a bitter anger*)   Oh, I marvel how such a strong man may let such a sickly wife be –

Proctor (*angered – at himself as well*)   You'll speak nothin' of Elizabeth!

Abigail   She is blackening my name in the village! She is telling lies about me! She is a cold, sniveling woman, and you bend to her! Let her turn you like a –

Proctor (*shaking her*)   Do you look for whippin'?

A psalm is heard being sung below.

Abigail (*in tears*)   I look for John Proctor that took me from my sleep and put knowledge in my heart! I never knew what pretense Salem was, I never knew the lying lessons I was taught by all these Christian women and their covenanted men! And now you bid me tear the light out of my eyes? I will not, I cannot! You loved me, John Proctor, and whatever sin it is, you love me yet! (*He turns abruptly to go out. She rushes to him.*) John, pity me, pity me!

The words 'going up to Jesus' are heard in the psalm, and **Betty** *claps her ears suddenly and whines loudly.*

Abigail   Betty? (*She hurries to* **Betty**, *who is now sitting up and screaming.* **Proctor** *goes to* **Betty** *as* **Abigail** *is trying to pull her hands down, calling 'Betty!'*)

Proctor (*growing unnerved*)   What's she doing? Girl, what ails you? Stop that wailing!

The singing has stopped in the midst of this, and now **Parris** *rushes in.*

Parris   What happened? What are you doing to her? Betty! (*He rushes to the bed, crying, 'Betty, Betty!'* **Mrs Putnam** *enters, feverish with curiosity, and with her* **Thomas Putnam** *and* **Mercy Lewis**. **Parris**, *at the bed, keeps lightly slapping* **Betty**'s *face, while she moans and tries to get up.*)

Abigail   She heard you singin' and suddenly she's up and screamin'.

Mrs Putnam   The psalm! The psalm! She cannot bear to hear the Lord's name!

Parris   No, God forbid. Mercy, run to the doctor! Tell him what's happened here! (**Mercy Lewis** *rushes out.*)

Mrs Putnam   Mark it for a sign, mark it!

Rebecca Nurse, *seventy-two, enters. She is white-haired, leaning upon her walking-stick.*

Putnam (*pointing at the whimpering* **Betty**)   That is a notorious sign of witchcraft afoot, Goody Nurse, a prodigious sign!

Mrs Putnam   My mother told me that! When they cannot bear to hear the name of –

Parris (*trembling*)   Rebecca, Rebecca, go to her, we're lost. She suddenly cannot bear to hear the Lord's –

Giles Corey, *eighty-three, enters. He is knotted with muscle, canny, inquisitive, and still powerful.*

Rebecca   There is hard sickness here, Giles Corey, so please to keep the quiet.

Giles   I've not said a word. No one here can testify I've said a word. Is she going to fly again? I hear she flies.

Putnam   Man, be quiet now!

Everything is quiet. **Rebecca** *walks across the room to the bed. Gentleness exudes from her.* **Betty** *is quietly whimpering, eyes shut.* **Rebecca** *simply stands over the child, who gradually quiets.*

And while they are so absorbed, we may put a word in for Rebecca. Rebecca was the wife of Francis Nurse, who, from all accounts, was one of those men for whom both sides of the argument had to have respect. He was called upon to arbitrate disputes as though he were an unofficial judge, and Rebecca also enjoyed the high opinion most people had for him. By the time of the delusion, they had three hundred acres, and their children were settled in separate homesteads within the same estate. However, Francis had originally rented the land, and one theory has it that, as he gradually paid for it and raised his social status, there were those who resented his rise.

Another suggestion to explain the systematic campaign against Rebecca, and inferentially against Francis, is the land war he fought with his neighbors, one of whom was a Putnam. This squabble grew to the proportions of a battle in the woods

between partisans of both sides, and it is said to have lasted
for two days. As for Rebecca herself, the general opinion of
her character was so high that to explain how anyone dared cry
her out for a witch – and more, how adults could bring
themselves to lay hands on her – we must look to the fields and
boundaries of that time.

As we have seen, Thomas Putnam's man for the Salem ministry was Bayley. The Nurse clan had been in the faction that pre-
vented Bayley's taking office. In addition, certain families allied
to the Nurses by blood or friendship, and whose farms were con-
tiguous with the Nurse farm or close to it, combined to break
away from the Salem town authority and set up Topsfield, a new
and independent entity whose existence was resented by old
Salemites.

That the guiding hand behind the outcry was Putnam's is
indicated by the fact that, as soon as it began, this Topsfield-
Nurse faction absented themselves from church in protest and
disbelief. It was Edward and Jonathan Putnam who signed the
first complaint against Rebecca; and Thomas Putnam's little
daughter was the one who fell into a fit at the hearing and
pointed to Rebecca as her attacker. To top it all, Mrs Putnam –
who is now staring at the bewitched child on the bed – soon
accused Rebecca's spirit of 'tempting her to iniquity', a charge
that had more truth in it than Mrs Putnam could know.

Mrs Putnam (*astonished*)   What have you done?

Rebecca, *in thought, now leaves the bedside and sits.*

Parris (*wondrous and relieved*)   What do you make of it,
Rebecca?

Putnam (*eagerly*)   Goody Nurse, will you go to my Ruth and
see if you can wake her?

Rebecca (*sitting*)   I think she'll wake in time. Pray calm
yourselves. I have eleven children, and I am twenty-six times a
grandma, and I have seen them all through their silly seasons,
and when it come on them they will run the Devil bowlegged
keeping up with their mischief. I think she'll wake when she

tires of it. A child's spirit is like a child, you can never catch it by running after it; you must stand still, and, for love, it will soon itself come back.

Proctor   Aye, that's the truth of it, Rebecca.

Mrs Putnam   This is no silly season, Rebecca. My Ruth is bewildered, Rebecca; she cannot eat.

Rebecca   Perhaps she is not hungered yet. (*To* **Parris**.) I hope you are not decided to go in search of loose spirits, Mr Parris. I've heard promise of that outside.

Parris   A wide opinion's running in the parish that the Devil may be among us, and I would satisfy them that they are wrong.

Proctor   Then let you come out and call them wrong. Did you consult the wardens before you called this minister to look for devils?

Parris   He is not coming to look for devils!

Proctor   Then what's he coming for?

Putnam   There be children dyin' in the village, Mister!

Proctor   I seen none dyin'. This society will not be a bag to swing around your head, Mr Putnam. (*To* **Parris**.) Did you call a meeting before you – ?

Putnam   I am sick of meetings; cannot the man turn his head without he have a meeting?

Proctor   He may turn his head, but not to Hell!

Rebecca   Pray, John, be calm. (*Pause. He defers to her.*) Mr Parris, I think you'd best send Reverend Hale back as soon as he come. This will set us all to arguin' again in the society, and we thought to have peace this year. I think we ought rely on the doctor now, and good prayer.

Mrs Putnam   Rebecca, the doctor's baffled!

Rebecca   If so he is, then let us go to God for the cause of it. There is prodigious danger in the seeking of loose spirits. I fear it, I fear it. Let us rather blame ourselves and –

Putnam   How may we blame ourselves? I am one of nine sons; the Putnam seed have peopled this province. And yet I have but one child left of eight – and now she shrivels!

Rebecca   I cannot fathom that.

Mrs Putnam (*with a growing edge of sarcasm*)   But I must! You think it God's work you should never lose a child, nor grandchild either, and I bury all but one? There are wheels within wheels in this village, and fires within fires!

Putnam (*to* **Parris**)   When Reverend Hale comes, you will proceed to look for signs of witchcraft here.

Proctor (*to* **Putnam**)   You cannot command Mr Parris. We vote by name in this society, not by acreage.

Putnam   I never heard you worried so on this society, Mr Proctor. I do not think I saw you at Sabbath meeting since snow flew.

Proctor   I have trouble enough without I come five mile to hear him preach only hellfire and bloody damnation. Take it to heart, Mr Parris. There are many others who stay away from church these days because you hardly ever mention God any more.

Parris (*now aroused*)   Why, that's a drastic charge!

Rebecca   It's somewhat true; there are many that quail to bring their children –

Parris   I do not preach for children, Rebecca. It is not the children who are unmindful of their obligations toward this ministry.

Rebecca   Are there really those unmindful?

Parris   I should say the better half of Salem village.

Putnam   And more than that!

Parris   Where is my wood? My contract provides I be supplied with all my firewood. I am waiting since November for a stick, and even in November I had to show my frostbitten hands like some London beggar!

Giles   You are allowed six pound a year to buy your wood, Mr Parris.

Parris   I regard that six pound as part of my salary. I am paid little enough without I spend six pound on firewood.

Proctor   Sixty, plus six for firewood –

Parris   The salary is sixty-six pound, Mr Proctor! I am not some preaching farmer with a book under my arm; I am a graduate of Harvard College.

Giles   Aye, and well instructed in arithmetic!

Parris   Mr Corey, you will look far for a man of my kind at sixty pound a year! I am not used to this poverty; I left a thrifty business in the Barbados to serve the Lord. I do not fathom it, why am I persecuted here? I cannot offer one proposition but there be a howling riot of argument. I have often wondered if the Devil be in it somewhere; I cannot understand you people otherwise.

Proctor   Mr Parris, you are the first minister ever did demand the deed to this house –

Parris   Man! Don't a minister deserve a house to live in?

Proctor   To live in, yes. But to ask ownership is like you shall own the meeting house itself; the last meeting I were at you spoke so long on deeds and mortgages I thought it were an auction.

Parris   I want a mark of confidence, is all! I am your third preacher in seven years. I do not wish to be put out like the cat whenever some majority feels the whim. You people seem not to comprehend that a minister is the Lord's man in the parish; a minister is not to be so lightly crossed and contradicted –

Putnam   Aye!

Parris   There is either obedience or the church will burn like Hell is burning!

Proctor   Can you speak one minute without we land in Hell again? I am sick of Hell!

Parris   It is not for you to say what is good for you to hear!

Proctor   I may speak my heart, I think!

Parris (*in a fury*)   What, are we Quakers? We are not Quakers here yet, Mr Proctor. And you may tell that to your followers!

Proctor   My followers!

Parris (*now he's out with it*)   There is a party in this church. I am not blind; there is a faction and a party.

Proctor   Against you?

Putnam   Against him and all authority!

Proctor   Why, then I must find it and join it.

There is shock among the others.

Rebecca   He does not mean that.

Putnam   He confessed it now!

Proctor   I mean it solemnly, Rebecca; I like not the smell of this 'authority'.

Rebecca   No, you cannot break charity with your minister. You are another kind, John. Clasp his hand, make your peace.

Proctor   I have a crop to sow and lumber to drag home. (*He goes angrily to the door and turns to* **Corey** *with a smile.*) What say you, Giles, let's find the party. He says there's a party.

Giles   I've changed my opinion of this man, John. Mr Parris, I beg your pardon. I never thought you had so much iron in you.

Parris (*surprised*)   Why, thank you, Giles!

Giles   It suggests to the mind what the trouble be among us all these years. (*To all.*) Think on it. Wherefore is everybody suing everybody else? Think on it now, it's a deep thing, and dark as a pit. I have been six time in court this year –

Proctor (*familiarly, with warmth, although he knows he is approaching the edge of* **Giles'** *tolerance with this*)   Is it the Devil's fault that a man cannot say you good morning without you clap him for defamation? You're old, Giles, and you're not hearin' so well as you did.

Giles (*he cannot be crossed*)   John Proctor, I have only last month collected four pound damages for you publicly sayin' I burned the roof off your house, and I –

Proctor (*laughing*)   I never said no such thing, but I've paid you for it, so I hope I can call you deaf without charge. Now come along, Giles, and help me drag my lumber home.

Putnam   A moment, Mr Proctor. What lumber is that you're draggin', if I may ask you?

Proctor   My lumber. From out my forest by the riverside.

Putnam   Why, we are surely gone wild this year. What anarchy is this? That tract is in my bounds, it's in my bounds, Mr Proctor.

Proctor   In your bounds! (*Indicating* **Rebecca**.) I bought that tract from Goody Nurse's husband five months ago.

Putnam   He had no right to sell it. It stands clear in my grandfather's will that all the land between the river and –

Proctor   Your grandfather had a habit of willing land that never belonged to him, if I may say it plain.

Giles   That's God's truth; he nearly willed away my north pasture but he knew I'd break his fingers before he'd set his name to it. Let's get your lumber home, John. I feel a sudden will to work coming on.

Putnam   You load one oak of mine and you'll fight to drag it home!

Giles   Aye, and we'll win too, Putnam – this fool and I. Come on! (*He turns to* **Proctor** *and starts out.*)

Putnam   I'll have my men on you, Corey! I'll clap a writ on you!

Enter **Reverend John Hale** *of Beverly.*

Mr Hale is nearing forty, a tight-skinned, eager-eyed intellectual. This is a beloved errand for him; on being called here to ascertain witchcraft he felt the pride of the specialist whose unique knowledge has at last been publicly called for. Like almost all men of learning, he spent a good deal of his time pondering the invisible world, especially since he had himself encountered a witch in his parish not long before. That woman, however, turned into a mere pest under his searching scrutiny, and the child she had allegedly been afflicting recovered her normal behavior after Hale had given her his kindness and a few days of rest in his own house. However, that experience never raised a doubt in his mind as to the reality of the underworld or the existence of Lucifer's many-faced lieutenants. And his belief is not to his discredit. Better minds than Hale's were – and still are – convinced that there is a society of spirits beyond our ken. One cannot help noting that one of his lines has never yet raised a laugh in any audience that has seen this play; it is his assurance that 'We cannot look to superstition in this. The Devil is precise.' Evidently we are not quite certain even now whether diabolism is holy and not to be scoffed at. And it is no accident that we should be so bemused.

Like Reverend Hale and the others on this stage, we conceive the Devil as a necessary part of a respectable view of cosmology. Ours is a divided empire in which certain ideas and emotions and actions are of God, and their opposites are of Lucifer. It is as impossible for most men to conceive of a morality without sin, as of an earth without 'sky'. Since 1692 a great but superficial change has wiped out God's beard and the Devil's horns, but the world is still gripped between two diametrically opposed absolutes. The concept of unity, in which positive and negative are attributes of the same force, in which good and evil are relative, ever-changing, and always joined to the same phenomenon – such a concept is still reserved to the physical sciences and to the few who have grasped the history of ideas. When it is recalled that until the Christian era the underworld was never regarded as a hostile area, that all gods were useful and essentially friendly to man despite occasional lapses; when we see the steady and methodical inculcation into humanity of the idea of man's worthlessness – until redeemed – the necessity of the Devil may become evident as a weapon, a weapon designed and used time and time again in every age to whip men into a surrender to a particular church or church-state.

Our difficulty in believing the – for want of a better word – political inspiration of the Devil is due in great part to the fact that he is called up and damned not only by our social antagonists but by our own side, whatever it may be. The Catholic Church, through its Inquisition, is famous for cultivating Lucifer as the arch-fiend, but the Church's enemies relied no less upon the Old Boy to keep the human mind enthralled. Luther was himself accused of alliance with Hell, and he in turn accused his enemies. To complicate matters further, he believed that he had had contact with the Devil and had argued theology with him. I am not surprised at this, for at my own university a professor of history – a Lutheran, by the way – used to assemble his graduate students, draw the shades, and commune in the classroom with Erasmus. He was never, to my knowledge, officially scoffed at for this, the reason being that the university officials, like most of us, are the children of a history which still sucks at the Devil's teats. At this writing, only England has held back before the temptations of contemporary diabolism. In the countries of the Communist ideology, all resistance of any import is linked to the totally malign capitalist succubi, and in America any man who is not reactionary in his views is open to the charge of alliance with the Red hell. Political opposition, thereby, is given an inhumane overlay which then justifies the abrogation of all normally applied customs of civilized intercourse. A political policy is equated with moral right, and opposition to it with diabolical malevolence. Once such an equation is effectively made, society becomes a congerie of plots and counterplots, and the main role of government changes from that of the arbiter to that of the scourge of God.

The results of this process are no different now from what they ever were, except sometimes in the degree of cruelty inflicted, and not always even in that department. Normally the actions and deeds of a man were all that society felt comfortable in judging. The secret intent of an action was left to the ministers, priests, and rabbis to deal with. When diabolism rises, however, actions are the least important manifests of the true nature of a man. The Devil, as Reverend Hale said, is a wily one, and, until an hour before he fell, even God thought him beautiful in Heaven.

The analogy, however, seems to falter when one considers that, while there were no witches then, there are Communists and capitalists now, and in each camp there is certain proof that spies of each side are at work undermining the other. But this is a snobbish objection and not at all warranted by the facts. I have no doubt that people *were* communing with, and even worshipping, the Devil in Salem, and if the whole truth could be known in this case, as it is in others, we should discover a regular and conventionalized propitiation of the dark spirit. One certain evidence of this is the confession of Tituba, the slave of Reverend Parris, and another is the behavior of the children who were known to have indulged in sorceries with her.

There are accounts of similar *klatches* in Europe, where the daughters of the towns would assemble at night and, sometimes with fetishes, sometimes with a selected young man, give themselves to love, with some bastardly results. The Church, sharp-eyed as it must be when gods long dead are brought to life, condemned these orgies as witchcraft and interpreted them, rightly, as a resurgence of the Dionysiac forces it had crushed long before. Sex, sin, and the Devil were early linked, and so they continued to be in Salem, and are today. From all accounts there are no more puritanical mores in the world than those enforced by the Communists in Russia, where women's fashions, for instance, are as prudent and all-covering as any American Baptist would desire! The divorce laws lay a tremendous responsibility on the father for the care of his children. Even the laxity of divorce regulations in the early years of the revolution was undoubtedly a revulsion from the nineteenth-century Victorian immobility of marriage and the consequent hypocrisy that developed from it. If for no other reasons, a state so powerful, so jealous of the uniformity of its citizens, cannot long tolerate the atomization of the family. And yet, in American eyes at least, there remains the conviction that the Russian attitude toward women is lascivious. It is the Devil working again, just as he is working within the Slav who is shocked at the very idea of a woman's disrobing herself in a burlesque show. Our opposites are always robed in sexual sin, and it is from this unconscious conviction that demonology gains both its attractive sensuality and its capacity to infuriate and frighten.

Coming into Salem now, Reverend Hale conceives of himself much as a young doctor on his first call. His painfully acquired armory of symptoms, catchwords, and diagnostic procedures are now to be put to use at last. The road from Beverly is unusually busy this morning, and he has passed a hundred rumors that make him smile at the ignorance of the yeomanry in this most precise science. He feels himself allied with the best minds of Europe – kings, philosophers, scientists, and ecclesiasts of all churches. His goal is light, goodness and its preservation, and he knows the exaltation of the blessed whose intelligence, sharpened by minute examinations of enormous tracts, is finally called upon to face what may be a bloody fight with the Fiend himself.

He appears loaded down with half a dozen heavy books.

Hale   Pray you, someone take these!

Parris (*delighted*)   Mr Hale! Oh! It's good to see you again! (*Taking some books.*) My, they're heavy!

Hale (*setting down his books*)   They must be; they are weighted with authority.

Parris (*a little scared*)   Well, you do come prepared!

Hale   We shall need hard study if it comes to tracking down the Old Boy. (*Noticing* **Rebecca**.) You cannot be Rebecca Nurse?

Rebecca   I am, sir. Do you know me?

Hale   It's strange how I knew you, but I suppose you look as such a good soul should. We have all heard of your great charities in Beverly.

Parris   Do you know this gentleman? Mr Thomas Putnam. And his good wife Ann.

Hale   Putnam! I had not expected such distinguished company, sir.

Putnam (*pleased*)   It does not seem to help us today, Mr Hale. We look to you to come to our house and save our child.

Hale   Your child ails too?

Mrs Putnam   Her soul, her soul seems flown away. She sleeps and yet she walks . . .

Putnam   She cannot eat.

Hale   Cannot eat! (*Thinks on it. Then, to* **Proctor** *and* **Giles Corey**.) Do you men have afflicted children?

Parris   No, no, these are farmers. John Proctor –

Giles Corey   He don't believe in witches.

Proctor (*to* **Hale**)   I never spoke on witches one way or the other. Will you come, Giles?

Giles   No – no, John, I think not. I have some few queer questions of my own to ask this fellow.

Proctor   I've heard you to be a sensible man, Mr Hale. I hope you'll leave some of it in Salem.

Proctor *goes.* **Hale** *stands embarrassed for an instant.*

Parris (*quickly*)   Will you look at my daughter, sir? (*Leads* **Hale** *to the bed.*) She has tried to leap out the window; we discovered her this morning on the highroad, waving her arms as though she'd fly.

Hale (*narrowing his eyes*)   Tries to fly.

Putnam   She cannot bear to hear the Lord's name, Mr Hale; that's a sure sign of witchcraft afloat.

Hale (*holding up his hands*)   No, no. Now let me instruct you. We cannot look to superstition in this. The Devil is precise; the marks of his presence are definite as stone, and I must tell you all that I shall not proceed unless you are prepared to believe me if I should find no bruise of hell upon her.

Parris   It is agreed, sir – it is agreed – we will abide by your judgment.

Hale   Good then. (*He goes to the bed, looks down at* **Betty**. *To* **Parris**.) Now, sir, what were your first warning of this strangeness?

Parris   Why, sir – I discovered *her* – (*indicating* **Abigail**) and my niece and ten or twelve of the other girls, dancing in the forest last night.

Hale (*surprised*)   You permit dancing?

Parris   No, no, it were secret –

Mrs Putnam (*unable to wait*)   Mr Parris's slave has knowledge of conjurin', sir.

Parris (*to* **Mrs Putnam**)   We cannot be sure of that, Goody Ann.

Mrs Putnam (*frightened, very softly*)   I know it, sir. I sent my child – she should learn from Tituba who murdered her sisters.

Rebecca (*horrified*)   Goody Ann! You sent a child to conjure up the dead?

Mrs Putnam   Let God blame me, not you, not you, Rebecca! I'll not have you judging me any more! (*To* **Hale**.) Is it a natural work to lose seven children before they live a day?

Parris   Sssh!

Rebecca, *with great pain, turns her face away. There is a pause.*

Hale   Seven dead in childbirth.

Mrs Putnam (*softly*)   Aye. (*Her voice breaks; she looks up at him. Silence.* **Hale** *is impressed.* **Parris** *looks to him. He goes to his books, opens one, turns pages, then reads. All wait, avidly.*)

Parris (*hushed*)   What book is that?

Mrs Putnam   What's there, sir?

Hale (*with a tasty love of intellectual pursuit*)   Here is all the invisible world, caught, defined, and calculated. In these books the Devil stands stripped of all his brute disguises. Here are all your familiar spirits – your incubi and succubi; your witches that go by land, by air, and by sea; your wizards of the night and of the day. Have no fear now – we shall find him out if he has come among us, and I mean to crush him utterly if he has shown his face! (*He starts for the bed.*)

Rebecca   Will it hurt the child, sir?

Hale   I cannot tell. If she is truly in the Devil's grip we may have to rip and tear to get her free.

Rebecca   I think I'll go, then. I am too old for this. (*She rises.*)

Parris (*striving for conviction*)   Why, Rebecca, we may open up the boil of all our troubles today!

Rebecca   Let us hope for that. I go to God for you, sir.

Parris (*with trepidation – and resentment*)   I hope you do not mean we go to Satan here! (*Slight pause.*)

Rebecca   I wish I knew. (*She goes out; they feel resentful of her note of moral superiority.*)

Putnam (*abruptly*)   Come, Mr Hale, let's get on. Sit you here.

Giles   Mr Hale, I have always wanted to ask a learned man – what signifies the readin' of strange books?

Hale   What books?

Giles   I cannot tell; she hides them.

Hale   Who does this?

Giles   Martha, my wife. I have waked at night many a time and found her in a corner, readin' of a book. Now what do you make of that?

Hale   Why, that's not necessarily –

Giles   It discomfits me! Last night – mark this – I tried and tried and could not say my prayers. And then she close her book and walks out of the house, and suddenly – mark this – I could pray again!

Old Giles must be spoken for, if only because his fate was to be so remarkable and so different from that of all the others. He was in his early eighties at this time, and was the most comical hero in the history. No man has ever been blamed for so much. If a cow was missed, the first thought was to look for her around Corey's house; a fire blazing up at night brought suspicion of arson to his door. He didn't give a hoot for public opinion, and only in his last years – after he had married Martha – did he bother much with the church. That she stopped his prayer is very probable, but he forgot to say that he'd only recently learned any prayers and it didn't take much to make him stumble over them. He was a crank and a nuisance, but withal a deeply innocent and brave man. In court, once, he was asked if it were true that he had been frightened by the strange behavior of a hog and had then said he knew it to be the Devil in an animal's shape. 'What frighted you?' he was asked. He forgot everything but the word 'frighted', and instantly replied, 'I do not know that I ever spoke that word in my life.'

Hale   Ah! The stoppage of prayer – that is strange. I'll speak further on that with you.

Giles   I'm not sayin' she's touched the Devil, now, but I'd admire to know what books she reads and why she hides them. She'll not answer me, y'see.

Hale   Aye, we'll discuss it. (*To all.*) Now mark me, if the Devil is in her you will witness some frightful wonders in this room, so please to keep your wits about you. Mr Putnam, stand close in case she flies. Now, Betty, dear, will you sit up? (**Putnam** *comes in closer, ready-handed.* **Hale** *sits* **Betty** *up, but she hangs limp in his hands.*) Hmmm. (*He observes her carefully. The others watch breathlessly.*) Can you hear me? I am John Hale, minister of Beverly. I have come to help you, dear. Do you remember my two little girls in Beverly? (*She does not stir in his hands.*)

Parris (*in fright*)   How can it be the Devil? Why would he choose my house to strike? We have all manner of licentious people in the village!

Hale   What victory would the Devil have to win a soul already bad? It is the best the Devil wants, and who is better than the minister?

Giles   That's deep, Mr Parris, deep, deep!

Parris (*with resolution now*)   Betty! Answer Mr Hale! Betty!

Hale   Does someone afflict you, child? It need not be a woman, mind you, or a man. Perhaps some bird invisible to others comes to you – Perhaps a pig, a mouse, or any beast at all. Is there some figure bids you fly? (*The child remains limp in his hands. In silence he lays her back on the pillow. Now, holding out his hands toward her, he intones.*) In nomine Domini Sabaoth sui filiique ite ad infernos. (*She does not stir. He turns to* **Abigail**, *his eyes narrowing.*) Abigail, what sort of dancing were you doing with her in the forest?

Abigail   Why – common dancing is all.

Parris   I think I ought to say that I – I saw a kettle in the grass where they were dancing.

Abigail   That were only soup.

Hale   What sort of soup were in this kettle, Abigail?

Abigail   Why, it were beans – and lentils, I think, and –

Hale   Mr Parris, you did not notice, did you, any living thing in the kettle? A mouse, perhaps, a spider, a frog – ?

Parris (*fearfully*)   I – do believe there were some movement – in the soup.

Abigail   That jumped in, we never put it in!

Hale (*quickly*)   What jumped in?

Abigail   Why, a very little frog jumped –

Parris   A frog, Abby!

Hale (*grasping* **Abigail**)   Abigail, it may be your cousin is dying. Did you call the Devil last night?

Abigail   I never called him! Tituba, Tituba . . .

Parris (*blanched*)   She called the Devil?

Hale   I should like to speak with Tituba.

Parris   Goody Ann, will you bring her up? (**Mrs Putnam** *exits*.)

Hale   How did she call him?

Abigail   I know not – she spoke Barbados.

Hale   Did you feel any strangeness when she called him? A sudden cold wind, perhaps? A trembling below the ground?

Abigail   I didn't see no Devil! (*Shaking* **Betty**.) Betty, wake up. Betty! Betty!

Hale   You cannot evade me, Abigail. Did your cousin drink any of the brew in that kettle?

Abigail   She never drank it.

Hale   Did you drink it?

Abigail   No, sir.

Hale   Did Tituba ask you to drink it?

Abigail   She tried, but I refused.

Hale   Why are you concealing? Have you sold yourself to Lucifer?

Abigail   I never sold myself! I'm a good girl! I'm a proper girl!

Mrs Putnam *enters with* **Tituba**, *and instantly* **Abigail** *points at* **Tituba**.

Abigail   She made me do it! She made Betty do it!

Tituba (*shocked and angry*)   Abby!

Abigail   She makes me drink blood!

Parris   Blood!!

Mrs Putnam   My baby's blood?

Tituba   No, no, chicken blood. I give she chicken blood!

Hale   Woman, have you enlisted these children for the Devil?

Tituba   No, no, sir, I don't truck with no Devil!

Hale   Why can she not wake? Are you silencing this child?

Tituba   I love me Betty!

Hale   You have sent your spirit out upon this child, have you not? Are you gathering souls for the Devil?

Abigail   She sends her spirit on me in church; she makes me laugh at prayer!

Parris   She have often laughed at prayer!

Abigail   She comes to me every night to go and drink blood!

Tituba   You beg *me* to conjure! She beg *me* make charm –

Abigail   Don't lie! (*To* **Hale**.) She comes to me while I sleep; she's always making me dream corruptions!

Tituba   Why you say that, Abby?

Abigail   Sometimes I wake and find myself standing in the open doorway and not a stitch on my body! I always hear her laughing in my sleep. I hear her singing her Barbados songs and tempting me with –

Tituba   Mister Reverend, I never –

Hale (*resolved now*)   Tituba, I want you to wake this child.

Tituba   I have no power on this child, sir.

Hale   You most certainly do, and you will free her from it now! When did you compact with the Devil?

Tituba   I don't compact with no Devil!

Parris   You will confess yourself or I will take you out and whip you to your death, Tituba!

Putnam   This woman must be hanged! She must be taken and hanged!

Tituba (*terrified, falls to her knees*)   No, no, don't hang Tituba! I tell him I don't desire to work for him, sir.

Parris   The Devil?

Hale   Then you saw him! (**Tituba** *weeps.*) Now Tituba, I know that when we bind ourselves to Hell it is very hard to break with it. We are going to help you tear yourself free –

Tituba (*frightened by the coming process*)   Mister Reverend, I do believe somebody else be witchin' these children.

Hale   Who?

Tituba   I don't know, sir, but the Devil got him numerous witches.

Hale   Does he! (*It is a clue.*) Tituba, look into my eyes. Come, look into me. (*She raises her eyes to his fearfully.*) You would be a good Christian woman, would you not, Tituba?

Tituba   Aye, sir, a good Christian woman.

Hale   And you love these little children?

Tituba   Oh, yes, sir, I don't desire to hurt little children.

Hale   And you love God, Tituba?

Tituba   I love God with all my bein'.

Hale   Now, in God's holy name –

Tituba   Bless Him. Bless Him. (*She is rocking on her knees, sobbing in terror.*)

Hale   And to His glory –

Tituba   Eternal glory. Bless Him – bless God . . .

Hale   Open yourself, Tituba – open yourself and let God's holy light shine on you.

Tituba   Oh, bless the Lord.

Hale   When the Devil comes to you does he ever come –
with another person? (*She stares up into his face.*) Perhaps another
person in the village? Someone you know.

Parris   Who came with him?

Putnam   Sarah Good? Did you ever see Sarah Good with
him? Or Osburn?

Parris   Was it man or woman came with him?

Tituba   Man or woman. Was – was woman.

Parris   What woman? A woman, you said. What woman?

Tituba   It was black dark, and I –

Parris   You could see him, why could you not see her?

Tituba   Well, they was always talking; they was always
runnin' round and carryin' on –

Parris   You mean out of Salem? Salem witches?

Tituba   I believe so, yes, sir.

Now **Hale** *takes her hand. She is surprised.*

Hale   Tituba. You must have no fear to tell us who they are,
do you understand? We will protect you. The Devil can never
overcome a minister. You know that, do you not?

Tituba (*kisses* **Hale***'s hand*)   Aye, sir, oh, I do.

Hale   You have confessed yourself to witchcraft, and that
speaks a wish to come to Heaven's side. And we will bless you,
Tituba.

Tituba (*deeply relieved*)   Oh, God bless you, Mr Hale!

Hale (*with rising exaltation*)   You are God's instrument put in
our hands to discover the Devil's agents among us. You are
selected, Tituba, you are chosen to help us cleanse our village.
So speak utterly, Tituba, turn your back on him and face God –
face God, Tituba, and God will protect you.

Tituba (*joining with him*)   Oh, God, protect Tituba!

Hale (*kindly*)   Who came to you with the Devil? Two? Three? Four? How many? (**Tituba** *pants, and begins rocking back and forth again, staring ahead.*)

Tituba   There was four. There was four.

Parris (*pressing in on her*)   Who? Who? Their names, their names!

Tituba (*suddenly bursting out*)   Oh, how many times he bid me kill you, Mr Parris!

Parris   Kill me!

Tituba (*in a fury*)   He say Mr Parris must be kill! Mr Parris no goodly man, Mr Parris mean man and no gentle man, and he bid me rise out of my bed and cut your throat! (*They gasp.*) But I tell him 'No! I don't hate that man. I don't want kill that man.' But he say, 'You work for me, Tituba, and I make you free! I give you pretty dress to wear, and put you way high up in the air, and you gone fly back to Barbados!' And I say, 'You lie, Devil, you lie!' And then he come one stormy night to me, and he say, 'Look! I have *white* people belong to me.' And I look – and there was Goody Good.

Parris   Sarah Good!

Tituba (*rocking and weeping*)   Aye, sir, and Goody Osburn.

Mrs Putnam   I knew it! Goody Osburn were midwife to me three times. I begged you, Thomas, did I not? I begged him not to call Osburn because I feared her. My babies always shriveled in her hands!

Hale   Take courage, you must give us all their names. How can you bear to see this child suffering? Look at her, Tituba. (*He is indicating* **Betty** *on the bed.*) Look at her God-given innocence; her soul is so tender; we must protect her, Tituba; the Devil is out and preying on her like a beast upon the flesh of the pure lamb. God will bless you for your help.

Abigail *rises, staring as though inspired, and cries out.*

Abigail I want to open myself! (*They turn to her, startled. She is enraptured, as though in a pearly light.*) I want the light of God, I want the sweet love of Jesus! I danced for the Devil; I saw him; I wrote in his book; I go back to Jesus; I kiss His hand. I saw Sarah Good with the Devil! I saw Goody Osburn with the Devil! I saw Bridget Bishop with the Devil!

As she is speaking, **Betty** *is rising from the bed, a fever in her eyes, and picks up the chant.*

Betty (*staring too*) I saw George Jacobs with the Devil! I saw Goody Howe with the Devil!

Parris She speaks! (*He rushes to embrace* **Betty**.) She speaks!

Hale Glory to God! It is broken, they are free!

Betty (*calling out hysterically and with great relief*) I saw Martha Bellows with the Devil!

Abigail I saw Goody Sibber with the Devil! (*It is rising to a great glee.*) The marshal, I'll call the marshal!

Parris *is shouting a prayer of thanksgiving.*

Betty I saw Alice Barrow with the Devil!

The curtain begins to fall.

Hale (*as* **Putnam** *goes out*) Let the marshal bring irons!

Abigail I saw Goody Hawkins with the Devil!

Betty I saw Goody Bibber with the Devil!

Abigail I saw Goody Booth with the Devil!

On their ecstatic cries –

Curtain.

Act Two

The common room of **Proctor***'s house, eight days later.*

At the right is a door opening on the fields outside. A fireplace is at the left, and behind it a stairway leading upstairs. It is the low, dark, and rather long living room of the time. As the curtain rises, the room is empty. From above, **Elizabeth** *is heard softly singing to the children. Presently the door opens and* **John Proctor** *enters, carrying his gun. He glances about the room as he comes toward the fireplace, then halts for an instant as he hears her singing. He continues on to the fireplace, leans the gun against the wall as he swings a pot out of the fire and smells it. Then he lifts out the ladle and tastes. He is not quite pleased. He reaches to a cupboard, takes a pinch of salt, and drops it into the pot. As he is tasting again, her footsteps are heard on the stair. He swings the pot into the fireplace and goes to a basin and washes his hands and face.* **Elizabeth** *enters.*

Elizabeth   What keeps you so late? It's almost dark.

Proctor   I were planting far out to the forest edge.

Elizabeth   Oh, you're done then.

Proctor   Aye, the farm is seeded. The boys asleep?

Elizabeth   They will be soon. (*And she goes to the fireplace, proceeds to ladle up stew in a dish.*)

Proctor   Pray now for a fair summer.

Elizabeth   Aye.

Proctor   Are you well today?

Elizabeth   I am. (*She brings the plate to the table, and, indicating the food:*) It is a rabbit.

Proctor (*going to the table*)   Oh, is it! In Jonathan's trap?

Elizabeth   No, she walked into the house this afternoon; I found her sittin' in the corner like she come to visit.

Proctor   Oh, that's a good sign walkin' in.

Elizabeth   Pray God. It hurt my heart to strip her, poor rabbit.

She sits and watches him taste it.

Proctor   It's well seasoned.

Elizabeth (*blushing with pleasure*)   I took great care. She's tender?

Proctor   Aye. (*He eats. She watches him.*) I think we'll see green fields soon. It's warm as blood beneath the clods.

Elizabeth   That's well.

Proctor *eats, then looks up.*

Proctor   If the crop is good I'll buy George Jacob's heifer. How would that please you?

Elizabeth   Aye, it would.

Proctor (*with a grin*)   I mean to please you, Elizabeth.

Elizabeth (*it is hard to say*)   I know it, John.

He gets up, goes to her, kisses her. She receives it. With a certain disappointment, he returns to the table.

Proctor (*as gently as he can*)   Cider?

Elizabeth (*with a sense of reprimanding herself for having forgot*) Aye! (*She gets up and goes and pours a glass for him. He now arches his back.*)

Proctor   This farm's a continent when you go foot by foot droppin' seeds in it.

Elizabeth (*coming with the cider*)   It must be.

Proctor (*drinks a long draught, then, putting the glass down*)   You ought to bring some flowers in the house.

Elizabeth   Oh! I forgot! I will tomorrow.

Proctor   It's winter in here yet. On Sunday let you come with me, and we'll walk the farm together; I never see such a load of flowers on the earth. (*With good feeling he goes and looks up* *at the sky through the open doorway.*) Lilacs have a purple smell. Lilac is the smell of nightfall, I think. Massachusetts is a beauty in the spring!

Elizabeth   Aye, it is.

There is a pause. She is watching him from the table as he stands there absorbing the night. It is as though she would speak but cannot. Instead, now, she takes up his plate and glass and fork and goes with them to the basin. Her back is turned to him. He turns to her and watches her. A sense of their separation rises.

Proctor   I think you're sad again. Are you?

Elizabeth (*she doesn't want friction, and yet she must*)   You come so late I thought you'd gone to Salem this afternoon.

Proctor   Why? I have no business in Salem.

Elizabeth   You did speak of going, earlier this week.

Proctor (*he knows what she means*)   I thought better of it since.

Elizabeth   Mary Warren's there today.

Proctor   Why'd you let her? You heard me forbid her go to Salem any more!

Elizabeth   I couldn't stop her.

Proctor (*holding back a full condemnation of her*)   It is a fault, it is a fault, Elizabeth – you're the mistress here, not Mary Warren.

Elizabeth   She frightened all my strength away.

Proctor   How may that mouse frighten you, Elizabeth? You –

Elizabeth   It is a mouse no more. I forbid her go, and she raises up her chin like the daughter of a prince and says to me, 'I must go to Salem, Goody Proctor; I am an official of the court!'

Proctor   Court! What court?

Elizabeth   Aye, it is a proper court they have now. They've sent four judges out of Boston, she says, weighty magistrates of the General Court, and at the head sits the Deputy Governor of the Province.

Proctor (*astonished*)   Why, she's mad.

Elizabeth   I would to God she were. There be fourteen people in the jail now, she says. (**Proctor** *simply looks at her, unable to grasp it.*) And they'll be tried, and the court have power to hang them too, she says.

Proctor (*scoffing, but without conviction*)   Ah, they'd never hang –

Elizabeth   The Deputy Governor promise hangin' if they'll not confess, John. The town's gone wild, I think. She speak of Abigail, and I thought she were a saint, to hear her. Abigail brings the other girls into the court, and where she walks the crowd will part like the sea for Israel. And folks are brought before them, and if they scream and howl and fall to the floor – the person's clapped in the jail for bewitchin' them.

Proctor (*wide-eyed*)   Oh, it is a black mischief.

Elizabeth   I think you must go to Salem, John. (*He turns to her.*) I think so. You must tell them it is a fraud.

Proctor (*thinking beyond this*)   Aye, it is, it is surely.

Elizabeth   Let you go to Ezekiel Cheever – he knows you well. And tell him what she said to you last week in her uncle's house. She said it had naught to do with witchcraft, did she not?

Proctor (*in thought*)   Aye, she did, she did. (*Now, a pause.*)

Elizabeth (*quietly, fearing to anger him by prodding*)   God forbid you keep that from the court, John. I think they must be told.

Proctor (*quietly, struggling with his thought*)   Aye, they must, they must. It is a wonder they do believe her.

Elizabeth   I would go to Salem now, John – let you go tonight.

Proctor   I'll think on it.

Elizabeth (*with her courage now*)   You cannot keep it, John.

Proctor (*angering*)   I know I cannot keep it. I say I will think on it!

Elizabeth (*hurt, and very coldly*)   Good, then, let you think on it. (*She stands and starts to walk out of the room.*)

Proctor   I am only wondering how I may prove what she told me, Elizabeth. If the girl's a saint now, I think it is not easy to prove she's fraud, and the town gone so silly. She told it to me in a room alone – I have no proof for it.

Elizabeth   You were alone with her?

Proctor (*stubbornly*)   For a moment alone, aye.

Elizabeth   Why, then, it is not as you told me.

Proctor (*his anger rising*)   For a moment, I say. The others come in soon after.

Elizabeth (*quietly – she has suddenly lost all faith in him*)   Do as you wish, then. (*She starts to turn.*)

Proctor   Woman. (*She turns to him.*) I'll not have your suspicion any more.

Elizabeth (*a little loftily*)   *I* have no –

Proctor   I'll not have it!

Elizabeth   Then let you not earn it.

Proctor (*with a violent undertone*)   You doubt me yet?

Elizabeth (*with a smile, to keep her dignity*)   John, if it were not Abigail that you must go to hurt, would you falter now? I think not.

Proctor   Now look you –

Elizabeth   I see what I see, John.

Proctor (*with solemn warning*)   You will not judge me more, Elizabeth. I have good reason to think before I charge fraud on Abigail, and I will think on it. Let you look to your own improvement before you go to judge your husband any more. I have forgot Abigail, and –

Elizabeth And I.

Proctor Spare me! You forget nothin' and forgive nothin'. Learn charity, woman. I have gone tiptoe in this house all seven month since she is gone. I have not moved from there to there without I think to please you, and still an everlasting funeral marches round your heart. I cannot speak but I am doubted, every moment judged for lies, as though I come into a court when I come into this house!

Elizabeth John, you are not open with me. You saw her with a crowd, you said. Now you –

Proctor I'll plead my honesty no more, Elizabeth.

Elizabeth (*now she would justify herself*) John, I am only –

Proctor No more! I should have roared you down when first you told me your suspicion. But I wilted, and, like a Christian, I confessed. Confessed! Some dream I had must have mistaken you for God that day. But you're not, you're not, and let you remember it! Let you look sometimes for the goodness in me, and judge me not.

Elizabeth I do not judge you. The magistrate sits in your heart that judges you. I never thought you but a good man, John – (*with a smile*) only somewhat bewildered.

Proctor (*laughing bitterly*) Oh, Elizabeth, your justice would freeze beer! (*He turns suddenly toward a sound outside. He starts for the door as* **Mary Warren** *enters. As soon as he sees her, he goes directly to her and grabs her by her cloak, furious.*) How do you go to Salem when I forbid it? Do you mock me? (*Shaking her.*) I'll whip you if you dare leave this house again!

Strangely, she doesn't resist him, but hangs limply by his grip.

Mary Warren I am sick, I am sick, Mr Proctor. Pray, pray, hurt me not. (*Her strangeness throws him off, and her evident pallor and weakness. He frees her.*) My insides are all shuddery; I am in the proceedings all day, sir.

Proctor (*with draining anger – his curiosity is draining it*) And what of these proceeding here? When will you proceed to keep this house, as you are paid nine pound a year to do – and my wife not wholly well?

As though to compensate, **Mary Warren** *goes to* **Elizabeth** *with a small rag doll.*

Mary Warren   I made a gift for you today, Goody Proctor. I had to sit long hours in a chair, and passed the time with sewing.

Elizabeth (*perplexed, looking at the doll*)   Why, thank you, it's a fair poppet.

Mary Warren (*with a trembling, decayed voice*)   We must all love each other now, Goody Proctor.

Elizabeth (*amazed at her strangeness*)   Aye, indeed we must.

Mary Warren (*glancing at the room*)   I'll get up early in the morning and clean the house. I must sleep now. (*She turns and starts off.*)

Proctor   Mary. (*She halts.*) Is it true? There be fourteen women arrested?

Mary Warren   No, sir. There be thirty-nine now – (*She suddenly breaks off and sobs and sits down, exhausted.*)

Elizabeth   Why, she's weepin'! What ails you, child?

Mary Warren   Goody Osburn – will hang!

There is a shocked pause, while she sobs.

Proctor   Hang! (*He calls into her face.*) Hang, y'say?

Mary Warren (*through her weeping*)   Aye.

Proctor   The Deputy Governor will permit it?

Mary Warren   He sentenced her. He must. (*To ameliorate it.*) But not Sarah Good. For Sarah Good confessed, y'see.

Proctor   Confessed! To what?

Mary Warren   That she – (*In horror at the memory.*) She sometimes made a compact with Lucifer, and wrote her name in his black book – with her blood – and bound herself to torment Christians till God's thrown down – and we all must worship Hell forevermore.

Pause.

Proctor But – surely you know what a jabberer she is. Did you tell them that?

Mary Warren Mr Proctor, in open court she near to choked us all to death.

Proctor How, choked you?

Mary Warren She sent her spirit out.

Elizabeth Oh, Mary, Mary, surely you –

Mary Warren (*with an indignant edge*) She tried to kill me many times, Goody Proctor!

Elizabeth Why, I never heard you mention that before.

Mary Warren I never knew it before. I never knew anything before. When she come into the court I say to myself, I must not accuse this woman, for she sleep in ditches, and so very old and poor. But then – then she sit there, denying and denying, and I feel a misty coldness climbin' up my back, and the skin on my skull begin to creep, and I feel a clamp around my neck and I cannot breathe air; and then – entranced – I hear a voice, a screamin' voice, and it were my voice – and all at once I remembered everything she done to me!

Proctor Why? What did she do to you?

Mary Warren (*like one awakened to a marvelous secret insight*) So many time, Mr Proctor, she come to this very door, beggin' bread and a cup of cider – and mark this: whenever I turned her away empty, she *mumbled*.

Elizabeth Mumbled! She may mumble if she's hungry.

Mary Warren But *what* does she mumble? You must remember, Goody Proctor. Last month – a Monday, I think – she walked away, and I thought my guts would burst for two days after. Do you remember it?

Elizabeth   Why – I do, I think, but –

Mary Warren   And so I told that to Judge Hathorne, and he asks her so. 'Goody Osburn,' says he, 'what curse do you mumble that this girl must fall sick after turning you away?' And then she replies – (*mimicking an old crone*) 'Why, your excellence, no curse at all. I only say my commandments; I hope I may say my commandments,' says she!

Elizabeth   And that's an upright answer.

Mary Warren   Aye, but then Judge Hathorne say, 'Recite for us your commandments!' – (*leaning avidly toward them*) and of all the ten she could not say a single one. She never knew no commandments, and they had her in a flat lie!

Proctor   And so condemned her?

Mary Warren   (*now a little strained, seeing his stubborn doubt*) Why, they must when she condemned herself.

Proctor   But the proof, the proof!

Mary Warren   (*with greater impatience with him*)   I told you the proof. It's hard proof, hard as rock, the judges said.

Proctor   (*pauses an instant, then*)   You will not go to court again, Mary Warren.

Mary Warren   I must tell you, sir, I will be gone every day now. I am amazed you do not see what weighty work we do.

Proctor   What work you do! It's strange work for a Christian girl to hang old women!

Mary Warren   But, Mr Proctor, they will not hang them if they confess. Sarah Good will only sit in jail some time – (*recalling*) and here's a wonder for you; think on this. Goody Good is pregnant!

Elizabeth   Pregnant! Are they mad? The woman's near to sixty!

Mary Warren   They had Doctor Griggs examine her, and she's full to the brim. And smokin' a pipe all these years, and no husband either! But she's safe, thank God, for they'll not hurt the innocent child. But be that not a marvel? You must see it, sir, it's God's work we do. So I'll be gone every day for some time: I am an official of the court, they say, and –

She has been edging toward offstage.

Proctor   I'll official you! (*He strides to the mantel, takes down the whip hanging there.*)

Mary Warren (*terrified, but coming erect, striving for her authority*) I'll not stand whipping any more!

Elizabeth (*hurriedly, as* **Proctor** *approaches*)   Mary, promise now you'll stay at home –

Mary Warren (*backing from him, but keeping her erect posture, striving, striving for her way*)   The Devil's loose in Salem, Mr Proctor; we must discover where he's hiding!

Proctor   I'll whip the Devil out of your (*With whip raised he reaches out for her, and she streaks away and yells.*)

Mary Warren (*pointing at* **Elizabeth**)   I saved her life today!

Silence. His whip comes down.

Elizabeth (*softly*)   I am accused?

Mary Warren (*quaking*)   Somewhat mentioned. But I said I never see no sign you ever sent your spirit out to hurt no one, and seeing I do live so closely with you, they dissmissed it.

Elizabeth   Who accused me?

Mary Warren   I am bound by law, I cannot tell it. (*To* **Proctor**.) I only hope you'll not be so sarcastical no more. Four judges and the King's deputy sat to dinner with us but an hour ago. I – I would have you speak civilly to me, from this out.

Proctor (*in horror, muttering in disgust at her*)   Go to bed.

Mary Warren (*with a stamp of her foot*)   I'll not be ordered to bed no more, Mr Proctor! I am eighteen and a woman, however single!

Proctor   Do you wish to sit up? Then sit up.

Mary Warren   I wish to go to bed!

Proctor (*in anger*)   Good night, then!

Mary Warren   Good night. (*Dissatisfied, uncertain of herself, she goes out. Wide-eyed, both,* **Proctor** *and* **Elizabeth** *stand staring.*)

Elizabeth (*quietly*)   Oh, the noose, the noose is up!

Proctor   There'll be no noose.

Elizabeth   She wants me dead. I knew all week it would come to this!

Proctor (*without conviction*)   They dismissed it. You heard her say –

Elizabeth   And what of tomorrow? She will cry me out until they take me!

Proctor   Sit you down.

Elizabeth   She wants me dead, John, you know it!

Proctor   I say sit down! (*She sits, trembling. He speaks quietly, trying to keep his wits.*) Now we must be wise, Elizabeth.

Elizabeth (*with sarcasm, and a sense of being lost*)   Oh, indeed, indeed!

Proctor   Fear nothing. I'll find Ezekiel Cheever. I'll tell him she said it were all sport.

Elizabeth   John, with so many in the jail, more than Cheever's help is needed now, I think. Would you favor me with this? Go to Abigail.

Proctor (*his soul hardening as he senses . . .*)   What have I to say to Abigail?

Elizabeth (*delicately*)   John – grant me this. You have a faulty understanding of young girls. There is a promise made in any bed –

Proctor (*striving against his anger*)   What promise?

Elizabeth   Spoke or silent, a promise is surely made. And she may dote on it now – I am sure she does – and thinks to kill me, then to take my place.

Proctor's *anger is rising; he cannot speak.*

Elizabeth   It is her dearest hope, John, I know it. There be a thousand names; why does she call mine? There be a certain danger in calling such a name – I am no Goody Good that sleeps in ditches, nor Osburn, drunk and half-witted. She'd dare not call out such a farmer's wife but there be monstrous profit in it. She thinks to take my place, John.

Proctor   She cannot think it! (*He knows it is true.*)

Elizabeth (*'reasonably'*)   John, have you ever shown her somewhat of contempt? She cannot pass you in the church but you will blush –

Proctor   I may blush for my sin.

Elizabeth   I think she sees another meaning in that blush.

Proctor   And what see you? What see you, Elizabeth?

Elizabeth (*'conceding'*)   I think you be somewhat ashamed, for I am there, and she so close.

Proctor   When will you know me, woman? Were I stone I would have cracked for shame this seven month!

Elizabeth   Then go and tell her she's a whore. Whatever promise she may sense – break it, John, break it.

Proctor (*between his teeth*)   Good, then. I'll go. (*He starts for his rifle.*)

Elizabeth (*trembling, fearfully*)   Oh, how unwillingly!

Proctor (*turning on her, rifle in hand*)   I will curse her hotter than the oldest cinder in hell. But pray, begrudge me not my anger!

Elizabeth   Your anger! I only ask you –

Proctor   Woman, am I so base? Do you truly think me base?

Elizabeth   I never called you base.

Proctor   Then how do you charge me with such a promise? The promise that a stallion gives a mare I gave that girl!

Elizabeth   Then why do you anger with me when I bid you break it?

Proctor   Because it speaks deceit, and I am honest! But I'll plead no more! I see now your spirit twists around the single error of my life, and I will never tear it free!

Elizabeth (*crying out*)   You'll tear it free – when you come to know that I will be your only wife, or no wife at all! She has an arrow in you yet, John Proctor, and you know it well!

Quite suddenly, as though from the air, a figure appears in the doorway. They start slightly. It is **Mr Hale**. *He is different now – drawn a little, and there is a quality of deference, even of guilt, about his manner now.*

Hale   Good evening.

Proctor (*still in his shock*)   Why, Mr Hale! Good evening to you, sir. Come in, come in.

Hale (*to* **Elizabeth**)   I hope I do not startle you.

Elizabeth   No, no, it's only that I heard no horse –

Hale   You are Goodwife Proctor.

Proctor   Aye; Elizabeth.

Hale (*nods, then*)   I hope you're not off to bed yet.

Proctor (*setting down his gun*)   No, no. (**Hale** *comes further into the room. And* **Proctor**, *to explain his nervousness.*) We are not used to visitors after dark, but you're welcome here. Will you sit you down, sir?

Hale   I will. (*He sits.*) Let you sit, Goodwife Proctor.

She does, never letting him out of her sight. There is a pause as **Hale** *looks about the room.*

Proctor (*to break the silence*)   Will you drink cider, Mr Hale?

Hale   No, it rebels my stomach; I have some further traveling yet tonight. Sit you down, sir. (**Proctor** *sits*.) I will not keep you long, but I have some business with you.

Proctor   Business of the court?

Hale   No – no, I come of my own, without the court's authority. Hear me. (*He wets his lips*.) I know not if you are aware, but your wife's name is – mentioned in the court.

Proctor   We know it, sir. Our Mary Warren told us. We are entirely amazed.

Hale   I am a stranger here, as you know. And in my ignorance I find it hard to draw a clear opinion of them that come accused before the court. And so this afternoon, and now tonight, I go from house to house – I come now from Rebecca Nurse's house and –

Elizabeth (*shocked*)   Rebecca's charged!

Hale   God forbid such a one be charged. She is, however – mentioned somewhat.

Elizabeth (*with an attempt at a laugh*)   You will never believe, I hope, that Rebecca trafficked with the Devil.

Hale   Woman, it is possible.

Proctor (*taken aback*)   Surely you cannot think so.

Hale   This is a strange time, Mister. No man may longer doubt the powers of the dark are gathered in monstrous attack upon this village. There is too much evidence now to deny it. You will agree, sir?

Proctor (*evading*)   I – have no knowledge in that line. But it's hard to think so pious a woman be secretly a Devil's bitch after seventy year of such good prayer.

Hale   Aye. But the Devil is a wily one, you cannot deny it. However, she is far from accused, and I know she will not be. (*Pause*.) I thought, sir, to put some questions as to the Christian character of this house, if you'll permit me.

Proctor (*coldly, resentful*)   Why, we have no fear of questions, sir.

Hale   Good, then. (*He makes himself more comfortable.*) In the book of record that Mr Parris keeps, I note that you are rarely in the church on Sabbath Day.

Proctor   No, sir, you are mistaken.

Hale   Twenty-six time in seventeen month, sir. I must call that rare. Will you tell me why you are so absent?

Proctor   Mr Hale, I never knew I must account to that man for I come to church or stay at home. My wife were sick this winter.

Hale   So I am told. But you, Mister, why could you not come alone?

Proctor   I surely did come when I could, and when I could not I prayed in this house.

Hale   Mr Proctor, your house is not a church; your theology must tell you that.

Proctor   It does, sir, it does; and it tells me that a minister may pray to God without he have golden candlesticks upon the altar.

Hale   What golden candlesticks?

Proctor   Since we built the church there were pewter candlesticks upon the altar; Francis Nurse made them, y'know, and a sweeter hand never touched the metal. But Parris came, and for twenty week he preach nothin' but golden candlesticks until he had them. I labor the earth from dawn of day to blink of night, and I tell you true, when I look to heaven and see my money glaring at his elbows – it hurt my prayer, sir, it hurt my prayer. I think, sometimes, the man dreams cathedrals, not clapboard meetin' houses.

Hale (*thinks, then*)   And yet, Mister, a Christian on Sabbath Day must be in church. (*Pause.*) Tell me – you have three children?

Proctor   Aye. Boys.

Hale   How comes it that only two are baptized?

Proctor (*starts to speak, then stops, then, as though unable to restrain this*)   I like it not that Mr Parris should lay his hand upon my baby. I see no light of God in that man. I'll not conceal it.

Hale   I must say it, Mr Proctor; that is not for you to decide. The man's ordained, therefore the light of God is in him.

Proctor (*flushed with resentment but trying to smile*)   What's your suspicion, Mr Hale?

Hale   No, no, I have no –

Proctor   I nailed the roof upon the church, I hung the door –

Hale   Oh, did you! That's a good sign, then.

Proctor   It may be I have been too quick to bring the man to book, but you cannot think we ever desired the destruction of religion. I think that's in your mind, is it not?

Hale (*not altogether giving way*)   I have – there is a softness in your record, sir, a softness.

Elizabeth   I think, maybe, we have been too hard with Mr Parris. I think so. But sure we never loved the Devil here.

Hale (*nods, deliberating this. Then, with the voice of one administering a secret test*)   Do you know your commandments, Elizabeth?

Elizabeth (*without hesitation, even eagerly*)   I surely do. There be no mark of blame upon my life, Mr Hale. I am a convenanted Christian woman.

Hale   And you, Mister?

Proctor (*a trifle unsteadily*)   I am sure I do, sir.

Hale (*glances at her open face, then at* **John**, *then*)   Let you repeat them, if you will.

Proctor   The commandments.

Hale   Aye.

Proctor (*looking out, beginning to sweat*)   Thou shalt not kill.

Hale   Aye.

Proctor (*counting on his fingers*)   Thou shalt not steal. Thou shalt not covet thy neighbor's goods, nor make unto thee any graven image. Thou shalt not take the name of the Lord in vain; thou shalt have no other gods before me. (*With some hesitation.*) Thou shalt remember the Sabbath Day and keep it holy. (*Pause. Then:*) Thou shalt honor thy father and mother. Thou shalt not bear false witness. (*He is stuck. He counts back on his fingers, knowing one is missing.*) Thou shalt not make unto thee any graven image.

Hale   You have said that twice, sir.

Proctor (*lost*)   Aye. (*He is flailing for it.*)

Elizabeth (*delicately*)   Adultery, John.

Proctor (*as though a secret arrow had pained his heart*)   Aye. (*Trying to grin it away – to* **Hale**.) You see, sir, between the two of us we do know them all. (**Hale** *only looks at* **Proctor**, *deep in his attempt to define this man.* **Proctor** *grows more uneasy.*) I think it be a small fault.

Hale   Theology, sir, is a fortress; no crack in a fortress may be accounted small. (*He rises; he seems worried now. He paces a little, in deep thought.*)

Proctor   There be no love for Satan in this house, Mister.

Hale   I pray it, I pray it dearly. (*He looks to both of them, an attempt at a smile on his face, but his misgivings are clear.*) Well, then – I'll bid you good night.

Elizabeth (*unable to restrain herself*)   Mr Hale. (*He turns.*) I do think you are suspecting me somewhat? Are you not?

Hale (*obviously disturbed – and evasive*)   Goody Proctor, I do not judge you. My duty is to add what I may to the godly wisdom of the court. I pray you both good health and good fortune. (*To* **John**.) Good night, sir. (*He starts out.*)

Elizabeth (*with a note of desperation*)   I think you must tell him, John.

Hale   What's that?

Elizabeth (*restraining a call*)   Will you tell him?

Slight pause. **Hale** *looks questioningly at* **John**.

Proctor (*with difficulty*)   I – I have no witness and cannot prove it . . . except my word be taken. But I know the children's sickness had naught to do with witchcraft.

Hale (*stopped, struck*)   Naught to do . . . ?

Proctor   Mr Parris discovered them sportin' in the woods. They startled and took sick.

Pause.

Hale   Who told you this?

Proctor (*hesitates, then*)   Abigail Williams.

Hale   Abigail!

Proctor   Aye.

Hale (*his eyes wide*)   Abigail Williams told you it had naught to do with witchcraft!

Proctor   She told me the day you came, sir.

Hale (*suspiciously*)   Why – why did you keep this?

Proctor   I never knew until tonight that the world is gone daft . . . with this nonsense.

Hale   Nonsense! Mister, I have myself examined Tituba, Sarah Good, and numerous others that have confessed to dealing with the Devil. They have *confessed* it.

Proctor   And why not, if they must hang for denying it? There are them that will swear to anything before they'll hang; have you never thought of that?

Hale   I have. I – I have indeed. (*It is his own suspicion, but he resists it. He glances at* **Elizabeth**, *then at* **John**.) And you . . . would you testify to this in court?

Proctor   I had not reckoned with goin' into court. But if I must, I will.

Hale   Do you falter here?

Proctor   I falter nothing, but I may wonder if my story will be credited in such a court. I do wonder on it, when such a steady-minded minister as you will suspicion such a woman that never lied, and cannot, and the world knows she cannot! I may falter somewhat, Mister; I am no fool.

Hale (*quietly – it has impressed him*)   Proctor, let you open with me now, for I have a rumor that troubles me. It's said you hold no belief that there may even be witches in the world. Is that true, sir?

Proctor (*he knows this is critical, and is striving against his disgust with* **Hale** *and with himself for even answering*)   I know not what I have said, I may have said it. I have wondered if there be witches in the world – although I cannot believe they come among us now.

Hale   Then you do not believe –

Proctor   I have no knowledge of it; the Bible speaks of witches, and I will not deny them.

Hale   And you, woman?

Elizabeth   I – I cannot believe it.

Hale (*shocked*)   You cannot!

Proctor   Elizabeth, you bewilder him!

Elizabeth (*to* **Hale**)   I cannot think the Devil may own a woman's soul, Mr Hale, when she keeps an upright way, as I have. I am a good woman, I know it; and if you believe I may do only good work in the world, and yet be secretly bound to Satan, then I must tell you, sir, I do not believe it.

Hale   But, woman, you do believe there are witches in –

Elizabeth   If you think that I am one, then I say there are none.

Hale   You surely do not fly against the Gospel, the Gospel –

Proctor   She believe in the Gospel, every word!

Elizabeth   Question Abigail Williams about the Gospel, not myself!

Hale *stares at her.*

Proctor   She do not mean to doubt the Gospel, sir, you cannot think it. This be a Christian house, sir, a Christian house.

Hale   God keep you both; let the third child be quickly baptized, and go you without fail each Sunday in to Sabbath prayer; and keep a solemn, quiet way among you. I think –

Giles Corey *appears in doorway.*

Giles   John!

Proctor   Giles! What's the matter?

Giles   They take my wife.

Francis Nurse *enters.*

Giles   And his Rebecca!

Proctor (*to* **Francis**)   Rebecca's in the *jail*!

Francis   Aye, Cheever come and take her in his wagon. We've only now come from the jail, and they'll not even let us in to see them.

Elizabeth   They've surely gone wild now, Mr Hale!

Francis (*going to* **Hale**)   Reverend Hale! Can you not speak to the Deputy Governor? I'm sure he mistakes these people –

Hale   Pray calm yourself, Mr Nurse.

Francis   My wife is the very brick and mortar of the church, Mr Hale – (*indicating* **Giles**) and Martha Corey, there cannot be a woman closer yet to God than Martha.

Hale   How is Rebecca charged, Mr Nurse?

Francis (*with a mocking, half-hearted laugh*)   For murder, she's charged! (*Mockingly quoting the warrant.*) 'For the marvelous and unnatural murder of Goody Putnam's babies.' What am I to do, Mr Hale?

Hale (*turns from* **Francis**, *deeply troubled, then*)   Believe me, Nurse, if Rebecca Nurse be tainted, then nothing's left to stop the whole green world from burning. Let you rest upon the justice of the court; the court will send her home, I know it.

Francis   You cannot mean she will be tried in court!

Hale (*pleading*)   Nurse, though our hearts break, we cannot flinch; these are new times, sir. There is a misty plot afoot so subtle we should be criminal to cling to old respects and ancient friendships. I have seen too many frightful proofs in court – the Devil is alive in Salem, and we dare not quail to follow wherever the accusing finger points!

Proctor (*angered*)   How may such a woman murder children?

Hale (*in great pain*)   Man, remember, until an hour before the Devil fell, God thought him beautiful in Heaven.

Giles   I never said my wife were a witch, Mr Hale; I only said she were reading books!

Hale   Mr Corey, exactly what complaint were made on your wife?

Giles   That bloody mongrel Walcott charge her. Y'see, he buy a pig of my wife four or five year ago, and the pig died soon after. So he come dancin' in for his money back. So my Martha, she says to him, 'Walcott, if you haven't the wit to feed a pig properly, you'll not live to own many,' she says. Now he goes to court and claims that from that day to this he cannot keep a pig alive for more than four weeks because my Martha bewitch them with her books!

Enter **Ezekiel Cheever**. *A shocked silence.*

Cheever   Good evening to you, Proctor.

Proctor   Why, Mr Cheever. Good evening.

Cheever   Good evening, all. Good evening, Mr Hale.

Proctor   I hope you come not on business of the court.

Cheever   I do, Proctor, aye. I am clerk of the court now, y'know.

Enter **Marshal Herrick**, *a man in his early thirties, who is somewhat shamefaced at the moment.*

Giles   It's a pity, Ezekiel, that an honest tailor might have gone to Heaven must burn in Hell. You'll burn for this, do you know it?

Cheever   You know yourself I must do as I'm told. You surely know that, Giles. And I'd as lief you'd not be sending me to Hell. I like not the sound of it, I tell you; I like not the sound of it. (*He fears* **Proctor**, *but starts to reach inside his coat.*) Now believe me, Proctor, how heavy be the law, all its tonnage I do carry on my back tonight. (*He takes out a warrant.*) I have a warrant for your wife.

Proctor (*to* **Hale**)   You said she were not charged!

Hale   I know nothin' of it. (*To* **Cheever**.) When were she charged?

Cheever   I am given sixteen warrant tonight, sir, and she is one.

Proctor   Who charged her?

Cheever   Why, Abigail Williams charge her.

Proctor   On what proof, what proof?

Cheever (*looking about the room*)   Mr Proctor, I have little time. The court bid me search your house, but I like not to search a house. So will you hand me any poppets that your wife may keep here?

Proctor   Poppets?

Elizabeth   I never kept no poppets, not since I were a girl.

Cheever (*embarrassed, glancing toward the mantel where sits* **Mary Warren**'s *poppet*)   I spy a poppet, Goody Proctor.

Elizabeth   Oh! (*Going for it.*) Why, this is Mary's.

Cheever (*shyly*)   Would you please to give it to me?

Elizabeth (*handing it to him, asks* **Hale**)   Has the court discovered a text in poppets now?

Cheever (*carefully holding the poppet*)   Do you keep any others in this house?

Proctor   No, nor this one either till tonight. What signifies a poppet?

Cheever   Why, a poppet – (*he gingerly turns the poppet over*) a poppet may signify – Now, woman, will you please to come with me?

Proctor   She will not! (*To* **Elizabeth**.) Fetch Mary here.

Cheever (*ineptly reaching toward* **Elizabeth**)   No, no, I am forbid to leave her from my sight.

Proctor (*pushing his arm away*)   You'll leave her out of sight and out of mind, Mister. Fetch Mary, Elizabeth. (**Elizabeth** *goes upstairs.*)

Hale   What signifies a poppet, Mr Cheever?

Cheever (*turning the poppet over in his hands*)   Why, they say it may signify that she – (*He has lifted the poppet's skirt, and his eyes widen in astonished fear.*) Why, this, this –

Proctor (*reaching for the poppet*)   What's there?

Cheever   Why – (*He draws out a long needle from the poppet.*) It is a needle! Herrick, Herrick, it is a needle!

Herrick *comes toward him.*

Proctor (*angrily, bewildered*)   And what signifies a needle!

Cheever (*his hands shaking*)   Why, this go hard with her, Proctor, this – I had my doubts, Proctor, I had my doubts, but here's a calamity. (*To* **Hale**, *showing the needle.*) You see it, sir, it is a needle!

Hale   Why? What meanin' has it?

Cheever (*wide-eyed, trembling*)   The girl, the Williams girl, Abigail Williams, sir. She sat to dinner in Reverend Parris's house tonight, and without word nor warnin' she falls to the floor. Like a struck beast, he says, and screamed a scream that a bull would weep to hear. And he goes to save her, and, stuck two inches in the flesh of her belly, he draw a needle out. And demandin' of her how she come to be so stabbed, she – (*to* **Proctor** *now*) testify it were your wife's familiar spirit pushed it in.

Proctor   Why, she done it herself! (*To* **Hale**.) I hope you're not takin' this for proof, Mister!

Hale, *struck by the proof, is silent.*

Cheever   'Tis hard proof! (*To* **Hale**.) I find here a poppet Goody Proctor keeps. I have found it, sir. And in the belly of the poppet, a needle's stuck. I tell you true, Proctor, I never warranted to see such proof of Hell, and I bid you obstruct me not, for I –

Enter **Elizabeth** *with* **Mary Warren**. **Proctor**, *seeing* **Mary Warren**, *draws her by the arm to* **Hale**.

Proctor   Here now! Mary, how did this poppet come into my house?

Mary Warren (*frightened for herself, her voice very small*)   What poppet's that, sir?

Proctor (*impatiently, pointing at the doll in* **Cheever**'s *hand*) This poppet, this poppet.

Mary Warren (*evasively, looking at it*)   Why, I – I think it mine.

Proctor   It is your poppet, is it not?

Mary Warren (*not understanding the direction of this*)   It is, sir.

Proctor   And how did it come into this house?

Mary Warren (*glancing about at the avid faces*)   Why – I made it in the court, sir, and give it to Goody Proctor tonight.

Proctor (*to* **Hale**)   Now, sir – do you have it?

Hale   Mary Warren, a needle have been found inside this poppet.

Mary Warren (*bewildered*)   Why, I meant no harm by it, sir.

Proctor (*quickly*)   You stuck that needle in yourself?

Mary Warren   I – I believe I did sir, I –

Proctor (*to* **Hale**)   What say you now?

Hale (*watching* **Mary Warren** *closely*)   Child, you are certain this be your natural memory? May it be, perhaps, that someone conjures you even now to say this?

Mary Warren   Conjures me? Why, no, sir, I am entirely myself, I think. Let you ask Susanna Walcott – she saw me sewin' it in court. (*Or better still.*) Ask Abby, Abby sat beside me when I made it.

Proctor (*to* **Hale**, *of* **Cheever**)   Bid him begone. Your mind is surely settled now. Bid him out, Mr Hale.

Elizabeth   What signifies a needle?

Hale   Mary – you charge a cold and cruel murder on Abigail.

Mary Warren   Murder! I charge no –

Hale   Abigail were stabbed tonight; a needle were found stuck into her belly –

Elizabeth   And she charges me?

Hale   Aye.

Elizabeth (*her breath knocked out*)   Why – ! The girl is murder! She must be ripped out of the world!

Cheever (*pointing at* **Elizabeth**)   You've heard that, sir! Ripped out of the world! Herrick, you heard it!

Proctor (*suddenly snatching the warrant out of* **Cheever**'*s hands*)
Out with you.

Cheever   Proctor, you dare not touch the warrant.

Proctor (*ripping the warrant*)   Out with you!

Cheever   You've ripped the Deputy Governor's warrant, man!

Proctor   Damn the Deputy Governor! Out of my house!

Hale   Now, Proctor, Proctor!

Proctor   Get y'gone with them! You are a broken minister.

Hale   Proctor, if she is innocent, the court –

Proctor   If she is innocent! Why do you never wonder if
Parris be innocent, or Abigail? Is the accuser always holy now?
Were they born this morning as clean as God's fingers? I'll tell
you what's walking Salem – vengeance is walking Salem. We
are what we always were in Salem, but now the little crazy
children are jangling the keys of the kingdom, and common
vengeance writes the law! This warrant's vengeance! I'll not
give my wife to vengeance!

Elizabeth   I'll go, John –

Proctor   You will not go!

Herrick   I have nine men outside. You cannot keep her. The
law binds me, John, I cannot budge.

Proctor (*to* **Hale**, *ready to break him*)   Will you see her taken?

Hale   Proctor, the court is just –

Proctor   Pontius Pilate! God will not let you wash your hands
of this!

Elizabeth   John – I think I must go with them. (*He cannot
bear to look at her.*) Mary, there is bread enough for the morning;
you will bake, in the afternoon. Help Mr Proctor as you were
his daughter – you owe me that, and much more. (*She is fighting
her weeping. To* **Proctor**.) When the children wake, speak
nothing of witchcraft – it will frighten them. (*She cannot go on.*)

Proctor   I will bring you home. I will bring you soon.

Elizabeth   Oh, John, bring me soon!

Proctor   I will fall like an ocean on that court! Fear nothing, Elizabeth.

Elizabeth (*with great fear*)   I will fear nothing. (*She looks about the room, as though to fix it in her mind.*) Tell the children I have gone to visit someone sick.

She walks out of the door, **Herrick** *and* **Cheever** *behind her. For a moment,* **Proctor** *watches from the doorway. The clank of chain is heard.*

Proctor   Herrick! Herrick, don't chain her! (*He rushes out the door. From outside.*) Damn you, man, you will not chain her! Off with them! I'll not have it! I will not have her chained!

There are other men's voices against his. **Hale**, *in a fever of guilt and uncertainty, turns from the door to avoid the sight;* **Mary Warren** *bursts into tears and sits weeping.* **Giles Corey** *calls to* **Hale**.

Giles   And yet silent, minister? It is fraud, you know it is fraud! What keeps you, man?

Proctor *is half braced, half pushed into the room by two deputies and* **Herrick**.

Proctor   I'll pay you, Herrick, I will surely pay you!

Herrick (*panting*)   In God's name, John, I cannot help myself. I must chain them all. Now let you keep inside this house till I am gone! (*He goes out with his deputies.*)

Proctor *stands there, gulping air. Horses and a wagon creaking are heard.*

Hale (*in great uncertainty*)   Mr Proctor –

Proctor   Out of my sight!

Hale   Charity, Proctor, charity. What I have heard in her favor, I will not fear to testify in court. God help me, I cannot judge her guilty or innocent – I know not. Only this consider:

the world goes mad, and it profit nothing you should lay the cause to the vengeance of a little girl.

Proctor   You are a coward! Though you be ordained in God's own tears, you are a coward now!

Hale   Proctor, I cannot think God be provoked so grandly by such a petty cause. The jails are packed – our greatest judges sit in Salem now – and hangin's promised. Man, we must look to cause proportionate. Were there murder done, perhaps, and never brought to light? Abomination? Some secret blasphemy that stinks to Heaven? Think on cause, man, and let you help me to discover it. For there's your way, believe it, there is your only way, when such confusion strikes upon the world. (*He goes to* **Giles** *and* **Francis**.) Let you counsel among yourselves; think on your village and what may have drawn from heaven such thundering wrath upon you all. I shall pray God open up our eyes.

Hale *goes out.*

Francis (*struck by* **Hale**'*s mood*)   I never heard no murder done in Salem.

Proctor (*he has been reached by* **Hale**'*s words*)   Leave me, Francis, leave me.

Giles (*shaken*)   John – tell me, are we lost?

Proctor   Go home now, Giles. We'll speak on it tomorrow.

Giles   Let you think on it. We'll come early, eh?

Proctor   Aye. Go now, Giles.

Giles   Good night, then.

Giles Corey *goes out. After a moment:*

Mary Warren (*in a fearful squeak of a voice*)   Mr Proctor, very likely they'll let her come home once they're given proper evidence.

Proctor   You're coming to the court with me, Mary. You will tell it in the court.

Mary Warren   I cannot charge murder on Abigail.

Proctor (*moving menacingly toward her*)   You will tell the court how that poppet come here and who stuck the needle in.

Mary Warren   She'll kill me for sayin' that! (**Proctor** *continues toward her.*) Abby'll charge lechery on you, Mr Proctor!

Proctor (*halting*)   She's told you!

Mary Warren   I have known it, sir. She'll ruin you with it, I know she will.

Proctor (*hesitating, and with deep hatred of himself*)   Good. Then her saintliness is done with. (**Mary** *backs from him.*) We will slide together into our pit; you will tell the court what you know.

Mary Warren (*in terror*)   I cannot, they'll turn on me –

Proctor *strides and catches her, and she is repeating, 'I cannot, I cannot!'*

Proctor   My wife will never die for me! I will bring your guts into your mouth but that goodness will not die for me!

Mary Warren (*struggling to escape him*)   I cannot do it, I cannot!

Proctor (*grasping her by the throat as though he would strangle her*) Make your peace with it! Now Hell and Heaven grapple on our backs, and all our old pretense is ripped away – make your peace! (*He throws her to the floor, where she sobs, 'I cannot, I cannot . . .' And now, half to himself, staring, and turning to the open door.*) Peace. It is a providence, and no great change; we are only what we always were, but naked now. (*He walks as though toward a great horror, facing the open sky.*) Aye, naked! And the wind, God's icy wind, will blow!

And she is over and over again sobbing, 'I cannot, I cannot, I cannot.'

Curtain.

Act Three

The vestry room of the Salem meeting house, now serving as the anteroom of the General Court.

As the curtain rises, the room is empty, but for sunlight pouring through two high windows in the back wall. The room is solemn, even forbidding. Heavy beams jut out, boards of random widths make up the walls. At the right are two doors leading into the meeting house proper, where the court is being held. At the left another door leads outside.

There is a plain bench at the left, and another at the right. In the center a rather long meeting table, with stools and a considerable armchair snugged up to it.

Through the partitioning wall at the right we hear a prosecutor's voice, **Judge Hathorne**'s, *asking a question; then a woman's voice,* **Martha Corey**'s, *replying.*

Hathorne's Voice   Now, Martha Corey, there is abundant evidence in our hands to show that you have given yourself to the reading of fortunes. Do you deny it?

Martha Corey's Voice   I am innocent to a witch. I know not what a witch is.

Hathorne's Voice   How do you know, then, that you are not a witch?

Martha Corey's Voice   If I were, I would know it.

Hathorne's Voice   Why do you hurt these children?

Martha Corey's Voice   I do not hurt them. I scorn it!

Giles's Voice (*roaring*)   I have evidence for the court!

Voices of townspeople rise in excitement.

Danforth's Voice   You will keep your seat!

Giles's Voice   Thomas Putnam is reaching out for land!

Danforth's Voice   Remove that man, Marshal!

Giles's Voice   You're hearing lies, lies!

A roaring goes up from the people.

Hathorne's Voice   Arrest him, Excellency!

Giles's Voice   I have evidence. Why will you not hear my evidence?

The door opens and **Giles** *is half carried into the vestry room by* **Herrick**.

Giles   Hands off, damn you, let me go!

Herrick   Giles, Giles!

Giles   Out of my way, Herrick! I bring evidence –

Herrick   You cannot go in there, Giles; it's a court!

Enter **Hale** *from the court.*

Hale   Pray be calm a moment.

Giles   You, Mr Hale, go in there and demand I speak.

Hale   A moment, sir, a moment.

Giles   They'll be hangin' my wife!

Judge Hathorne *enters. He is in his sixties, a bitter, remorseless Salem judge.*

Hathorne   How do you dare come roarin' into this court! Are you gone daft, Corey?

Giles   You're not a Boston judge yet, Hathorne. You'll not call me daft!

Enter **Deputy Governor Danforth** *and, behind him,* **Ezekiel Cheever** *and* **Parris**. *On his appearance, silence falls.* **Danforth** *is a grave man in his sixties, of some humor and sophistication that does not, however, interfere with an exact loyalty to his position and his cause. He comes down to* **Giles**, *who awaits his wrath.*

Danforth (*looking directly at* **Giles**)   Who is this man?

Parris   Giles Corey, sir, and a more contentious –

Giles (*to* **Parris**)   I am asked the question, and I am old enough to answer it! (*To* **Danforth**, *who impresses him and to whom he smiles through his strain.*) My name is Corey, sir, Giles Corey. I have six hundred acres, and timber in addition. It is my wife you be condemning now. (*He indicates the courtroom.*)

Danforth   And how do you imagine to help her cause with such contemptuous riot? Now be gone. Your old age alone keeps you out of jail for this.

Giles (*beginning to plead*)   They be tellin' lies about my wife, sir, I –

Danforth   Do you take it upon yourself to determine what this court shall believe and what it shall set aside?

Giles   Your Excellency, we mean no disrespect for –

Danforth   Disrespect indeed! It is disruption, Mister. This is the highest court of the supreme government of this province, do you know it?

Giles (*beginning to weep*)   Your Excellency, I only said she were readin' books, sir, and they come and take her out of my house for –

Danforth (*mystified*)   Books! What books?

Giles (*through helpless sobs*)   It is my third wife, sir; I never had no wife that be so taken with books, and I thought to find the cause of it, d'y'see, but it were no witch I blamed her for. (*He is openly weeping.*) I have broke charity with the woman, I have broke charity with her. (*He covers his face, ashamed.* **Danforth** *is respectfully silent.*)

Hale   Excellency, he claims hard evidence for his wife's defense. I think that in all justice you must –

Danforth   Then let him submit his evidence in proper affidavit. You are certainly aware of our procedure here, Mr Hale. (*To* **Herrick**.) Clear this room.

Herrick   Come now, Giles. (*He gently pushes* **Corey** *out.*)

Francis   We are desperate, sir; we come here three days now and cannot be heard.

Danforth   Who is this man?

Francis   Francis Nurse, Your Excellency.

Hale   His wife's Rebecca that were condemned this morning.

Danforth   Indeed! I am amazed to find you in such uproar. I have only good report of your character, Mr Nurse.

Hathorne   I think they must both be arrested in contempt, sir.

Danforth (*to* **Francis**)   Let you write your plea, and in due time I will –

Francis   Excellency, we have proof for your eyes; God forbid you shut them to it. The girls, sir, the girls are frauds.

Danforth   What's that?

Francis   We have proof of it, sir. They are all deceiving you.

Danforth *is shocked, but studying* **Francis**.

Hathorne   This is contempt, sir, contempt!

Danforth   Peace, Judge Hathorne. Do you know who I am, Mr Nurse?

Francis   I surely do, sir, and I think you must be a wise judge to be what you are.

Danforth   And do you know that near to four hundred are in the jails from Marblehead to Lynn, and upon my signature?

Francis   I –

Danforth   And seventy-two condemned to hang by that signature?

Francis   Excellency, I never thought to say it to such a weighty judge, but you are deceived.

Enter **Giles Corey** *from left. All turn to see as he beckons in* **Mary Warren** *with* **Proctor**. **Mary** *is keeping her eyes to the ground;* **Proctor** *has her elbow as though she were near collapse.*

Parris (*on seeing her, in shock*)   Mary Warren! (*He goes directly to bend close to her face.*) What are you about here?

Proctor (*pressing* **Parris** *away from her with a gentle but firm motion of protectiveness*)   She would speak with the Deputy Governor.

Danforth (*shocked by this, turns to* **Herrick**)   Did you not tell me Mary Warren were sick in bed?

Herrick   She were, Your Honor. When I go to fetch her to the court last week, she said she were sick.

Giles   She has been strivin' with her soul all week, Your Honor; she comes now to tell the truth of this to you.

Danforth   Who is this?

Proctor   John Proctor, sir. Elizabeth Proctor is my wife.

Parris   Beware this man, Your Excellency, this man is mischief.

Hale (*excitedly*)   I think you must hear the girl, sir, she –

Danforth (*who has become very interested in* **Mary Warren** *and only raises a hand toward* **Hale**)   Peace. What would you tell us, Mary Warren?

Proctor *looks at her, but she cannot speak.*

Proctor   She never saw no spirits, sir.

Danforth (*with great alarm and surprise, to* **Mary**)   Never saw no spirits!

Giles (*eagerly*)   Never.

Proctor (*reaching into his jacket*)   She has signed a deposition, sir –

Danforth (*instantly*)   No, no, I accept no depositions. (*He is rapidly calculating this; he turns from her to* **Proctor**.) Tell me, Mr Proctor, have you given out this story in the village?

Proctor   We have not.

Parris   They've come to overthrow the court, sir! This man is –

Danforth   I pray you, Mr Parris. Do you know, Mr Proctor, that the entire contention of the state in these trials is that the voice of Heaven is speaking through the children?

Proctor   I know that, sir.

Danforth (*thinks, staring at* **Proctor**, *then turns to* **Mary Warren**) And you, Mary Warren, how came you to cry out people for sending their spirits against you?

Mary Warren   It were pretense, sir.

Danforth   I cannot hear you.

Proctor   It were pretense, she says.

Danforth   Ah? And the other girls? Susanna Walcott, and the others? They are also pretending?

Mary Warren   Aye, sir.

Danforth (*wide-eyed*)   Indeed. (*Pause. He is baffled by this. He turns to study* **Proctor**'*s face.*)

Parris (*in a sweat*)   Excellency, you surely cannot think to let so vile a lie be spread in open court!

Danforth   Indeed not, but it strike hard upon me that she will dare come here with such a tale. Now, Mr Proctor, before I decide whether I shall hear you or not, it is my duty to tell you this. We burn a hot fire here; it melts down all concealment.

Proctor   I know that, sir.

Danforth   Let me continue. I understand well, a husband's tenderness may drive him to extravagance in defense of a wife. Are you certain in your conscience, Mister, that your evidence is the truth?

Proctor   It is. And you will surely know it.

Danforth   And you thought to declare this revelation in the open court before the public?

Proctor   I thought I would, aye – with your permission.

Danforth (*his eyes narrowing*)   Now, sir, what is your purpose in so doing?

Proctor   Why, I – I would free my wife, sir.

Danforth   There lurks nowhere in your heart, nor hidden in your spirit, any desire to undermine this court?

Proctor (*with the faintest faltering*)   Why, no, sir.

Cheever (*clears his throat, awakening*)   I – Your Excellency.

Danforth   Mr Cheever.

Cheever   I think it be my duty, sir – (*Kindly, to* **Proctor**.) You'll not deny it, John. (*To* **Danforth**.) When we come to take his wife, he damned the court and ripped your warrant.

Parris   Now you have it!

Danforth   He did that, Mr Hale?

Hale (*takes a breath*)   Aye, he did.

Proctor   It were a temper, sir. I knew not what I did.

Danforth (*studying him*)   Mr Proctor.

Proctor   Aye, sir.

Danforth (*straight into his eyes*)   Have you ever seen the Devil?

Proctor   No, sir.

Danforth   You are in all respects a Gospel Christian?

Proctor   I am, sir.

Parris   Such a Christian that will not come to church but once in a month!

Danforth (*restrained – he is curious*)   Not come to church?

Proctor   I – I have no love for Mr Parris. It is no secret. But God I surely love.

Cheever   He plow on Sunday, sir.

Danforth   Plow on Sunday!

Cheever (*apologetically*)   I think it be evidence, John. I am an official of the court, I cannot keep it.

Proctor   I – I have once or twice plowed on Sunday. I have three children, sir, and until last year my land give little.

Giles   You'll find other Christians that do plow on Sunday if the truth be known.

Hale   Your Honor, I cannot think you may judge the man on such evidence.

Danforth   I judge nothing. (*Pause. He keeps watching* **Proctor**, *who tries to meet his gaze.*) I tell you straight, Mister – I have seen marvels in this court. I have seen people choked before my eyes by spirits; I have seen them stuck by pins and slashed by daggers. I have until this moment not the slightest reason to suspect that the children may be deceiving me. Do you understand my meaning?

Proctor   Excellency, does it not strike upon you that so many of these women have lived so long with such upright reputation, and –

Parris   Do you read the Gospel, Mr Proctor?

Proctor   I read the Gospel.

Parris   I think not, or you should surely know that Cain were an upright man, and yet he did kill Abel.

Proctor   Aye, God tells us that. (*To* **Danforth**.) But who tells us Rebecca Nurse murdered seven babies by sending out her spirit on them? It is the children only, and this one will swear she lied to you.

Danforth *considers, then beckons* **Hathorne** *to him.* **Hathorne** *leans in, and he speaks in his ear.* **Hathorne** *nods.*

Hathorne   Aye, she's the one.

Danforth   Mr Proctor, this morning, your wife send me a claim in which she states that she is pregnant now.

Proctor   My wife pregnant!

Danforth   There be no sign of it – we have examined her body.

Proctor   But if she say she is pregnant, then she must be! That woman will never lie, Mr Danforth.

Danforth   She will not?

Proctor   Never, sir, never.

Danforth   We have thought it too convenient to be credited. However, if I should tell you now that I will let her be kept another month; and if she begin to show her natural signs, you shall have her living yet another year until she is delivered – what say you to that? (**John Proctor** *is struck silent.*) Come now. You say your only purpose is to save your wife. Good, then, she is saved at least this year, and a year is long. What say you, sir? It is done now. (*In conflict,* **Proctor** *glances at* **Francis** *and* **Giles**.) Will you drop this charge?

Proctor   I – I think I cannot.

Danforth (*now an almost imperceptible hardness in his voice*)   Then your purpose is somewhat larger.

Parris   He's come to overthrow this court, Your Honor!

Proctor   These are my friends. Their wives are also accused –

Danforth (*with a sudden briskness of manner*)   I judge you not, sir. I am ready to hear your evidence.

Proctor   I come not to hurt the court; I only –

Danforth (*cutting him off*)   Marshal, go into the court and bid Judge Stoughton and Judge Sewall declare recess for one hour. And let them go to the tavern, if they will. All witnesses and prisoners are to be kept in the building.

Herrick   Aye, sir. (*Very deferentially.*) If I may say it, sir, I know this man all my life. It is a good man, sir.

Danforth (*it is the reflection on himself he resents*)   I am sure of it, Marshal. (**Herrick** *nods, then goes out.*) Now, what deposition do you have for us, Mr Proctor? And I beg you be clear, open as the sky, and honest.

Proctor (*as he takes out several papers*)   I am no lawyer, so I'll –

Danforth   The pure in heart need no lawyers. Proceed as you will.

Proctor (*handing* **Danforth** *a paper*)   Will you read this first, sir? It's a sort of testament. The people signing it declare their good opinion of Rebecca, and my wife, and Martha Corey. (**Danforth** *looks down at the paper.*)

Parris (*to enlist* **Danforth**'*s sarcasm*)   Their good opinion! (*But* **Danforth** *goes on reading, and* **Proctor** *is heartened.*)

Proctor   These are all landholding farmers, members of the church. (*Delicately, trying to point out a paragraph.*) If you'll notice, sir – they've known the women many years and never saw no sign they had dealings with the Devil.

Parris *nervously moves over and reads over* **Danforth**'*s shoulder.*

Danforth (*glancing down a long list*)   How many names are here?

Francis   Ninety-one, Your Excellency.

Parris (*sweating*)   These people should be summoned. (**Danforth** *looks up at him questioningly.*) For questioning.

Francis (*trembling with anger*)   Mr Danforth, I gave them all my word no harm would come to them for signing this.

Parris   This is a clear attack upon the court!

Hale (*to* **Parris**, *trying to contain himself*)   Is every defense an attack upon the court? Can no one – ?

Parris   All innocent and Christian people are happy for the courts in Salem! These people are gloomy for it. (*To* **Danforth** *directly.*) And I think you will want to know, from each and every one of them, what discontents them with you!

Hathorne   I think they ought to be examined, sir.

Danforth   It is not necessarily an attack, I think. Yet –

Francis   These are all covenanted Christians, sir.

Danforth   Then I am sure they may have nothing to fear. (*Hands* **Cheever** *the paper.*) Mr Cheever, have warrants drawn for all of these – arrest for examination. (*To* **Proctor**.) Now, Mister, what information do you have for us? (**Francis** *is still standing, horrified.*) You may sit, Mr Nurse.

Francis   I have brought trouble on these people; I have –

Danforth   No, old man, you have not hurt these people if they are of good conscience. But you must understand, sir, that a person is either with this court or he must be counted against it, there be no road between. This is a sharp time, now, a precise time – we live no longer in the dusky afternoon when evil mixed itself with good and befuddled the world. Now, by God's grace, the shining sun is up, and them that fear not light will surely praise it. I hope you will be one of those. (**Mary Warren** *suddenly sobs.*) She's not hearty I see.

Proctor   No, she's not, sir. (*To* **Mary**, *bending to her, holding her hand, quietly.*) Now remember what the angel Raphael said to the boy Tobias. Remember it.

Mary Warren (*hardly audible*)   Aye.

Proctor   'Do that which is good, and no harm shall come to thee.'

Mary Warren   Aye.

Danforth   Come, man, we wait you.

Marshal Herrick *returns, and takes his post at the door.*

Giles   John, my deposition, give him mine.

Proctor   Aye. (*He hands* **Danforth** *another paper.*) This is Mr Corey's deposition.

Danforth   Oh? (*He looks down at it. Now* **Hathorne** *comes behind him and reads with him.*)

Hathorne (*suspiciously*)   What lawyer drew this, Corey?

Giles   You know I never hired a lawyer in my life, Hathorne.

Danforth (*finishing the reading*)   It is very well phrased. My compliments. Mr Parris, if Mr Putnam is in the court, will you bring him in? (**Hathorne** *takes the deposition, and walks to the window with it.* **Parris** *goes into the court.*) You have no legal training, Mr Corey?

Giles (*very pleased*)   I have the best, sir – I am thirty-three time in court in my life. And always plaintiff, too.

Danforth   Oh, then you're much put-upon.

Giles   I am never put-upon; I know my rights, sir, and I will have them. You know, your father tried a case of mine – might be thirty-five year ago, I think.

Danforth   Indeed.

Giles   He never spoke to you of it?

Danforth   No, I cannot recall it.

Giles   That's strange, he give me nine pound damages. He were a fair judge, your father. Y'see, I had a white mare that time, and this fellow come to borrow the mare – (*Enter* **Parris** *with* **Thomas Putnam**. *When he sees* **Putnam**, **Giles**'s *ease goes; he is hard.*) Aye, there he is.

Danforth   Mr Putnam, I have here an accusation by Mr Corey against you. He states that you coldly prompted your daughter to cry witchery upon George Jacobs that is now in jail.

Putnam   It is a lie.

Danforth (*turning to* **Giles**)   Mr Putnam states your charge is a lie. What say you to that?

Giles (*furious, his fists clenched*)   A fart on Thomas Putnam, that is what I say to that!

Danforth   What proof do you submit for your charge, sir?

Giles   My proof is there! (*Pointing to the paper.*) If Jacobs hangs for a witch he forfeit up his property – that's law! And there is none but Putnam with the coin to buy so great a piece. This man is killing his neighbors for their land!

Danforth   But proof, sir, proof.

Giles (*pointing at his deposition*)   The proof is there! I have it from an honest man who heard Putnam say it! The day his daughter cried out on Jacobs, he said she'd given him a fair gift of land.

Hathorne   And the name of this man?

Giles (*taken aback*)   What name?

Hathorne   The man that give you this information.

Giles (*hesitates, then*)   Why, I – I cannot give you his name.

Hathorne   And why not?

Giles (*hesitates, then bursts out*)   You know well why not! He'll lay in jail if I give his name!

Hathorne   This is contempt of the court, Mr Danforth!

Danforth (*to avoid that*)   You will surely tell us the name.

Giles   I will not give you no name. I mentioned my wife's name once and I'll burn in hell long enough for that. I stand mute.

Danforth   In that case, I have no choice but to arrest you for contempt of this court, do you know that?

Giles   This is a hearing; you cannot clap me for contempt of a hearing.

Danforth   Oh, it is a proper lawyer! Do you wish me to declare the court in full session here? Or will you give me good reply?

Giles (*faltering*)   I cannot give you no name, sir, I cannot.

Danforth   You are a foolish old man. Mr Cheever, begin the record. The court is now in session. I ask you, Mr Corey –

Proctor (*breaking in*)   Your Honor – he has the story in confidence, sir, and he –

Parris   The Devil lives on such confidences! (*To* **Danforth**.) Without confidences there could be no conspiracy, Your Honor!

Hathorne   I think it must be broken, sir.

Danforth (*to* **Giles**)   Old man, if your informant tells the truth let him come here openly like a decent man. But if he hide in anonymity I must know why. Now sir, the government and central church demand of you the name of him who reported Mr Thomas Putnam a common murderer.

Hale   Excellency –

Danforth   Mr Hale.

Hale   We cannot blink it more. There is a prodigious fear of this court in the country –

Danforth   Then there is a prodigious guilt in the country. Are *you* afraid to be questioned here?

Hale   I may only fear the Lord, sir, but there is fear in the country nevertheless.

Danforth (*angered now*)   Reproach me not with the fear in the country; there is fear in the country because there is a moving plot to topple Christ in the country!

Hale   But it does not follow that everyone accused is part of it.

Danforth   No uncorrupted man may fear this court, Mr Hale! None! (*To* **Giles**.) You are under arrest in contempt of this court. Now sit you down and take counsel with yourself, or you will be set in the jail until you decide to answer all questions.

Giles Corey *makes a rush for* **Putnam**. **Proctor** *lunges and holds him.*

Proctor   No, Giles!

Giles (*over* **Proctor**'s *shoulder at* **Putnam**)   I'll cut your throat, Putnam, I'll kill you yet!

Proctor (*forcing him into a chair*) Peace, Giles, peace. (*Releasing him.*) We'll prove ourselves. Now we will. (*He starts to turn to* **Danforth**.)

Giles Say nothin' more, John. (*Pointing at* **Danforth**.) He's only playin' you! You means to hang us all!

Mary Warren *bursts into sobs.*

Danforth This is a court of law, Mister. I'll have no effrontery here!

Proctor Forgive him, sir, for his old age. Peace, Giles, we'll prove it all now. (*He lifts up* **Mary**'s *chin.*) You cannot weep, Mary. Remember the angel, what he say to the boy. Hold to it, now; there is your rock. (**Mary** *quiets. He takes out a paper, and turns to* **Danforth**.) This is Mary Warren's deposition. I – I would ask you remember, sir, while you read it, that until two week ago she were no different than the other children are today. (*He is speaking reasonably, restraining all his fears, his anger, his anxiety.*) You saw her scream, she howled, she swore familiar spirits choked her; she even testified that Satan, in the form of women now in jail, tried to win her soul away, and then when she refused –

Danforth We know all this.

Proctor Aye, sir. She swears now that she never saw Satan; nor any spirit, vague or clear, that Satan may have sent to hurt her. And she declares her friends are lying now.

Proctor *starts to hand* **Danforth** *the deposition, and* **Hale** *comes up to* **Danforth** *in a trembling state.*

Hale Excellency, a moment. I think this goes to the heart of the matter.

Danforth (*with deep misgivings*) It surely does.

Hale I cannot say he is an honest man; I know him little. But in all justice, sir, a claim so weighty cannot be argued by a farmer. In God's name, sir, stop here; send him home and let him come again with a lawyer –

Danforth (*patiently*) Now look you, Mr Hale –

Hale   Excellency, I have signed seventy-two death warrants; I am a minister of the Lord, and I dare not take a life without there be a proof so immaculate no slightest qualm of conscience may doubt it.

Danforth   Mr Hale, you surely do not doubt my justice.

Hale   I have this morning signed away the soul of Rebecca Nurse, Your Honor. I'll not conceal it, my hand shakes yet as with a wound! I pray you, sir, *this* argument let lawyers present to you.

Danforth   Mr Hale, believe me; for a man of such terrible learning you are most bewildered – I hope you will forgive me. I have been thirty-two year at the bar, sir, and I should be confounded were I called upon to defend these people. Let you consider, now – (*To* **Proctor** *and the others.*) And I bid you all do likewise. In an ordinary crime, how does one defend the accused? One calls up witnesses to prove his innocence. But witchcraft is *ipso facto*, on its face and by its nature, an invisible crime, is it not? Therefore, who may possibly be witness to it? The witch and the victim. None other. Now we cannot hope the witch will accuse herself; granted? Therefore, we must rely upon her victims – and they do testify, the children certainly do testify. As for the witches, none will deny that we are most eager for all their confessions. Therefore, what is left for a lawyer to bring out? I think I have made my point. Have I not?

Hale   But this child claims the girls are not truthful, and if they are not –

Danforth   That is precisely what I am about to consider, sir. What more may you ask of me? Unless you doubt my probity?

Hale (*defeated*)   I surely do not, sir. Let you consider it, then.

Danforth   And let you put your heart to rest. Her deposition, Mr Proctor.

Proctor *hands it to him.* **Hathorne** *rises, goes beside* **Danforth**, *and starts reading.* **Parris** *comes to his other side.* **Danforth** *looks at* **John Proctor**, *then proceeds to read.* **Hale** *gets up, finds position near the judge, reads too.* **Proctor** *glances at* **Giles**. **Francis** *prays* *silently, hands pressed together.* **Cheever** *waits placidly, the sublime official, dutiful.* **Mary Warren** *sobs once.* **John Proctor** *touches her head reassuringly. Presently* **Danforth** *lifts his eyes, stands up, takes out a kerchief and blows his nose. The others stand aside as he moves in thought toward the window.*

Parris (*hardly able to contain his anger and fear*)   I should like to question –

Danforth (*his first real outburst, in which his contempt for* **Parris** *is clear*)   Mr Parris, I bid you be silent! (*He stands in silence, looking out the window. Now, having established that he will set the gait:*) Mr Cheever, will you go into the court and bring the children here? (**Cheever** *gets up and goes out upstage.* **Danforth** *now turns to* **Mary**.) Mary Warren, how came you to this turnabout? Has Mr Proctor threatened you for this deposition?

Mary Warren   No, sir.

Danforth   Has he ever threatened you?

Mary Warren (*weaker*)   No, sir.

Danforth (*sensing a weakening*)   Has he threatened you?

Mary Warren   No, sir.

Danforth   Then you tell me that you sat in my court, callously lying, when you knew that people would hang by your evidence? (*She does not answer.*) Answer me!

Mary Warren (*almost inaudibly*)   I did, sir.

Danforth   How were you instructed in your life? Do you not know that God damns all liars? (*She cannot speak.*) Or is it now that you lie?

Mary Warren   No, sir – I am with God now.

Danforth   You are with God now.

Mary Warren   Aye, sir.

Danforth (*containing himself*)   I will tell you this – you are either lying now, or you were lying in the court, and in either case you have committed perjury and you will go to jail for it. You cannot lightly say you lied, Mary. Do you know that?

Mary Warren   I cannot lie no more. I am with God, I am with God.

But she breaks into sobs at the thought of it, and the right door opens, and enter **Susanna Walcott**, **Mercy Lewis**, **Betty Parris**, *and finally* **Abigail**. **Cheever** *comes to* **Danforth**.

Cheever   Ruth Putnam's not in the court, sir, nor the other children.

Danforth   These will be sufficient. Sit you down, children. (*Silently they sit.*) Your friend, Mary Warren, has given us a deposition. In which she swears that she never saw familiar spirits, apparitions, nor any manifest of the Devil. She claims as well that none of you have seen these things either. (*Slight pause.*) Now, children, this is a court of law. The law, based upon the Bible, and the Bible, writ by Almighty God, forbid the practice of witchcraft, and describe death as the penalty thereof. But likewise, children, the law and Bible damn all bearers of false witness. (*Slight pause.*) Now then. It does not escape me that this deposition may be devised to blind us; it may well be that Mary Warren has been conquered by Satan, who sends her here to distract our sacred purpose. If so, her neck will break for it. But if she speak true, I bid you now drop your guile and confess your pretense, for a quick confession will go easier with you. (*Pause.*) Abigail Williams, rise. (**Abigail** *slowly rises.*) Is there any truth in this?

Abigail   No, sir.

Danforth (*thinks, glances at* **Mary**, *then back to* **Abigail**) Children, a very augur bit will now be turned into your souls until your honesty is proved. Will either of you change your positions now, or do you force me to hard questioning?

Abigail   I have naught to change, sir. She lies.

Danforth (*to* **Mary**)   You would still go on with this?

Mary Warren (*faintly*)   Aye, sir.

Danforth (*turning to* **Abigail**)   A poppet were discovered in Mr Proctor's house, stabbed by a needle. Mary Warren claims that you sat beside her in the court when she made it, and that you saw her make it and witnessed how she herself stuck her needle into it for safe-keeping. What say you to that?

Abigail (*with a slight note of indignation*)   It is a lie, sir.

Danforth (*after a slight pause*)   While you worked for Mr Proctor, did you see poppets in that house?

Abigail   Goody Proctor always kept poppets.

Proctor   Your Honor, my wife never kept no poppets. Mary Warren confesses it was her poppet.

Cheever   Your Excellency.

Danforth   Mr Cheever.

Cheever   When I spoke with Goody Proctor in that house, she said she never kept no poppets. But she said she did keep poppets when she were a girl.

Proctor   She has not been a girl these fifteen years, Your Honor.

Hathorne   But a poppet will keep fifteen years, will it not?

Proctor   It will keep if it is kept, but Mary Warren swears she never saw no poppets in my house, nor anyone else.

Parris   Why could there not have been poppets hid where no one ever saw them?

Proctor (*furious*)   There might also be a dragon with five legs in my house, but no one has ever seen it.

Parris   We are here, Your Honor, precisely to discover what no one has ever seen.

Proctor   Mr Danforth, what profit this girl to turn herself about? What may Mary Warren gain but hard questioning and worse?

Danforth   You are charging Abigail Williams with a marvelous cool plot to murder, do you understand that?

Proctor   I do, sir. I believe she means to murder.

Danforth (*pointing at* **Abigail**, *incredulously*)   This child would murder your wife?

Proctor   It is not a child. Now hear me, sir. In the sight of the congregation she were twice this year put out of this meetin' house for laughter during prayer.

Danforth (*shocked, turning to* **Abigail**)   What's this? Laughter during – !

Parris   Excellency, she were under Tituba's power at that time, but she is solemn now.

Giles   Aye, now she is solemn and goes to hang people!

Danforth   Quiet, man.

Hathorne   Surely it have no bearing on the question, sir. He charges contemplation of murder.

Danforth   Aye. (*He studies* **Abigail** *for a moment, then:*) Continue, Mr Proctor.

Proctor   Mary. Now tell the Governor how you danced in the woods.

Parris (*instantly*)   Excellency, since I come to Salem this man is blackening my name. He –

Danforth   In a moment, sir. (*To* **Mary Warren**, *sternly, and surprised.*) What is this dancing?

Mary Warren   I – (*She glances at* **Abigail**, *who is staring down at her remorselessly. Then, appealing to* **Proctor**.) Mr Proctor –

Proctor (*taking it right up*)   Abigail leads the girls to the woods, Your Honor, and they have danced there naked –

Parris   Your Honor, this –

Proctor (*at once*)   Mr Parris discovered them himself in the dead of night! There's the 'child' she is!

Danforth (*it is growing into a nightmare, and he turns, astonished, to* **Parris**)   Mr Parris –

Parris   I can only say, sir, that I never found any of them naked, and this man is –

Danforth   But you discovered them dancing in the woods? (*Eyes on* **Parris***, he points at* **Abigail**.) Abigail?

Hale   Excellency, when I first arrived from Beverly, Mr Parris told me that.

Danforth   Do you deny it, Mr Parris?

Parris   I do not, sir, but I never saw any of them naked.

Danforth   But she have *danced*?

Parris (*unwillingly*)   Aye, sir.

Danforth*, as though with new eyes, looks at* **Abigail**.

Hathorne   Excellency, will you permit me? (*He points at* **Mary Warren**.)

Danforth (*with great worry*)   Pray, proceed.

Hathorne   You say you never saw no spirits, Mary, were never threatened or afflicted by any manifest of the Devil or the Devil's agents.

Mary Warren (*very faintly*)   No, sir.

Hathorne (*with a gleam of victory*)   And yet, when people accused of witchery confronted you in court, you would faint, saying their spirits came out of their bodies and choked you –

Mary Warren   That were pretense, sir.

Danforth   I cannot hear you.

Mary Warren   Pretense, sir.

Parris   But you did turn cold, did you not? I myself picked you up many times, and your skin were icy. Mr Danforth, you –

Danforth   I saw that many times.

Proctor   She only pretended to faint, Your Excellency. They're all marvelous pretenders.

Hathorne   Then can she pretend to faint now?

Proctor   Now?

Parris   Why not? Now there are no spirits attacking her, for none in this room is accused of witchcraft. So let her turn herself cold now, let her pretend she is attacked now, let her faint. (*He turns to* **Mary Warren**.) Faint!

Mary Warren   Faint?

Parris   Aye, faint. Prove to us how you pretended in the court so many times.

Mary Warren (*looking to* **Proctor**)   I cannot faint now, sir.

Proctor (*alarmed, quietly*)   Can you not pretend it?

Mary Warren   I – (*She looks about as though searching for the passion to faint.*) I have no *sense* of it now. I –

Danforth   Why? What is lacking now?

Mary Warren   I cannot tell, sir, I –

Danforth   Might it be that here we have no afflicting spirit loose, but in the court there were some?

Mary Warren   I never saw no spirits.

Parris   Then see no spirits now, and prove to us that you can faint by your own will, as you claim.

Mary Warren (*stares, searching for the emotion of it, and then shakes her head*)   I cannot do it.

Parris   Then you will confess, will you not? It were attacking spirits made you faint!

Mary Warren   No, sir, I –

Parris   Your Excellency, this is a trick to blind the court!

Mary Warren   It's not a trick! (*She stands.*) I – I used to faint because I – I thought I saw spirits.

Danforth   *Thought* you saw them!

Mary Warren   But I did not, Your Honor.

Hathorne   How could you think you saw them unless you saw them?

Mary Warren   I – I cannot tell how, but I did. I – I heard the other girls screaming, and you, Your Honor, you seemed to believe them, and I – It were only sport in the beginning, sir, but then the whole world cried spirits, spirits, and I – I promise you, Mr Danforth, I only thought I saw them but I did not.

Danforth *peers at her.*

Parris (*smiling, but nervous because* **Danforth** *seems to be struck by* **Mary Warren***'s story*)   Surely Your Excellency is not taken by this simple lie.

Danforth (*turning worriedly to* **Abigail**)   Abigail. I bid you now search your heart and tell me this – and beware of it, child, to God every soul is precious and His vengeance is terrible on them that take life without cause. Is it possible, child, that the spirits you have seen are illusion only, some deception that may cross your mind when –

Abigail   Why, this – this is a base question, sir.

Danforth   Child, I would have you consider it –

Abigail   I have been hurt, Mr Danforth; I have seen my blood runnin' out! I have been near to murdered every day because I done my duty pointing out the Devil's people – and this is my reward? To be mistrusted, denied, questioned like a –

Danforth (*weakening*)   Child, I do not mistrust you –

Abigail (*in an open threat*)   Let *you* beware, Mr Danforth. Think you to be so mighty that the power of Hell may not turn *your* wits? Beware of it! There is – (*Suddenly, from an accusatory attitude, her face turns, looking into the air above – it is truly frightened.*)

Danforth (*apprehensively*)   What is it, child?

Abigail (*looking about in the air, clasping her arms about her as though cold*)   I – I know not. A wind, a cold wind, has come. (*Her eyes fall on* **Mary Warren**.)

Mary Warren (*terrified, pleading*)   Abby!

Mercy Lewis (*shivering*)   Your Honor, I freeze!

Proctor   They're pretending!

Hathorne (*touching* **Abigail**'s *hand*)   She is cold, Your Honor, touch her!

Mercy Lewis (*through chattering teeth*)   Mary, do you send this shadow on me?

Mary Warren   Lord, save me!

Susanna Walcott   I freeze, I freeze!

Abigail (*shivering visibly*)   It is a wind, a wind!

Mary Warren   Abby, don't do that!

Danforth (*himself engaged and entered by* **Abigail**)   Mary Warren, do you witch her? I say to you, do you send your spirit out?

With a hysterical cry **Mary Warren** *starts to run.* **Proctor** *catches her.*

Mary Warren (*almost collapsing*)   Let me go, Mr Proctor, I cannot, I cannot –

Abigail (*crying to Heaven*)   Oh, Heavenly Father, take away this shadow!

Without warning or hesitation, **Proctor** *leaps at* **Abigail** *and, grabbing her by the hair, pulls her to her feet. She screams in pain.* **Danforth**, *astonished, cries, 'What are you about?' and* **Hathorne** *and* **Parris** *call, 'Take your hands off her!' and out of it all comes* **Proctor**'s *roaring voice.*

Proctor   How do you call Heaven! Whore! Whore!

Herrick *breaks* **Proctor** *from her.*

Herrick   John!

Danforth   Man! Man, what do you –

Proctor (*breathless and in agony*)   It is a whore!

Danforth (*dumbfounded*)   You charge – ?

Abigail   Mr Danforth, he is lying!

Proctor   Mark her! Now she'll suck a scream to stab me with but –

Danforth   You will prove this! This will not pass!

Proctor (*trembling, his life collapsing about him*)   I have known her, sir. I have known her.

Danforth   You – you are a lecher?

Francis (*horrified*)   John, you cannot say such a –

Proctor   Oh, Francis, I wish you had some evil in you that you might know me! (*To* **Danforth**.) A man will not cast away his good name. You surely know that.

Danforth (*dumbfounded*)   In – in what time? In what place?

Proctor (*his voice about to break, and his shame great*)   In the proper place – where my beasts are bedded. On the last night of my joy, some eight months past. She used to serve me in my house, sir. (*He has to clamp his jaw to keep from weeping.*) A man may think God sleeps, but God sees everything, I know it now. I beg you, sir, I beg you – see her what she is. My wife, my dear good wife, took this girl soon after, sir, and put her out on the highroad. And being what she is, a lump of vanity, sir – (*He is being overcome.*) Excellency, forgive me, forgive me. (*Angrily, against himself, he turns away from the Governor for a moment. Then, as though to cry out is his only means of speech left:*) She thinks to dance with me on my wife's grave! And well she might, for I thought of her softly. God help me, I lusted, and there *is* a promise in such sweat. But it is a whore's vengeance, and you must see it; I set myself entirely in your hands. I know you must see it now.

Danforth (*blanched, in horror, turning to* **Abigail**)   You deny every scrap and tittle of this?

Abigail   If I must answer that, I will leave and I will not come back again!

Danforth *seems unsteady.*

Proctor   I have made a bell of my honor! I have rung the doom of my good name – you will believe me, Mr Danforth! My wife is innocent, except she knew a whore when she saw one!

Abigail (*stepping up to* **Danforth**)   What look do you give me? (**Danforth** *cannot speak.*) I'll not have such looks! (*She turns and starts for the door.*)

Danforth   You will remain where you are! (**Herrick** *steps into her path. She comes up short, fire in her eyes.*) Mr Parris, go into the court and bring Goodwife Proctor out.

Parris (*objecting*)   Your Honor, this is all a –

Danforth (*sharply to* **Parris**)   Bring her out! And tell her not one word of what's been spoken here. And let you knock before you enter. (**Parris** *goes out.*) Now we shall touch the bottom of this swamp. (*To* **Proctor**.) Your wife, you say, is an honest woman.

Proctor   In her life, sir, she have never lied. There are them that cannot sing, and them that cannot weep – my wife cannot lie. I have paid much to learn it, sir.

Danforth   And when she put this girl out of your house, she put her out for a harlot?

Proctor   Aye, sir.

Danforth   And knew her for a harlot?

Proctor   Aye, sir, she knew her for a harlot.

Danforth   Good then. (*To* **Abigail**.) And if she tell me, child, it were for harlotry, may God spread His mercy on you! (*There is a knock. He calls to the door.*) Hold! (*To* **Abigail**.) Turn your back. Turn your back. (*To* **Proctor**.) Do likewise. (*Both turn their backs* – **Abigail** *with indignant slowness.*) Now let neither of you turn to face Goody Proctor. No one in this room is to speak one word, or raise a gesture aye or nay. (*He turns toward the door, calls.*) Enter! (*The door opens.* **Elizabeth** *enters with* **Parris**. **Parris** *leaves her. She stands alone, her eyes looking for* **Proctor**.) Mr Cheever, report this testimony in all exactness. Are you ready?

Cheever   Ready, sir.

Danforth   Come here, woman. (**Elizabeth** *comes to him, glancing at* **Proctor**'*s back.*) Look at me only, not at your husband. In my eyes only.

Elizabeth (*faintly*)   Good, sir.

Danforth   We are given to understand that at one time you dismissed your servant, Abigail Williams.

Elizabeth   That is true, sir.

Danforth   For what cause did you dismiss her? (*Slight pause. Then* **Elizabeth** *tries to glance at* **Proctor**.) You will look in my eyes only and not at your husband. The answer is in your memory and you need no help to give it to me. Why did you dismiss Abigail Williams?

Elizabeth (*not knowing what to say, sensing a situation, wetting her lips to stall for time.*)   She – dissatisfied me. (*Pause.*) And my husband.

Danforth   In what way dissatisfied you?

Elizabeth   She were – (*She glances at* **Proctor** *for a cue.*)

Danforth   Woman, look at me! (**Elizabeth** *does.*) Were she slovenly? Lazy? What disturbance did she cause?

Elizabeth   Your Honor, I – in that time I were sick. And my husband is a good and righteous man. He is never drunk as some are, nor wastin' his time at the shovelboard, but always at his work. But in my sickness – you see, sir, I were a long time sick after my last baby, and I thought I saw my husband somewhat turning from me. And this girl – (*She turns to* **Abigail**.)

Danforth   Look at me.

Elizabeth   Aye, sir. Abigail Williams – (*She breaks off.*)

Danforth   What of Abigail Williams?

Elizabeth   I came to think he fancied her. And so one night I lost my wits, I think, and put her out on the highroad.

Danforth   Your husband – did he indeed turn from you?

Elizabeth (*in agony*)   My husband – is a goodly man, sir.

Danforth   Then he did not turn from you.

Elizabeth (*starting to glance at* **Proctor**)   He –

Danforth (*reaches out and holds her face, then*)   Look at me! To your own knowledge, has John Proctor ever committed the crime of lechery? (*In a crisis of indecision she cannot speak.*) Answer my question! Is your husband a lecher!

Elizabeth (*faintly*)   No, sir.

Danforth   Remove her, Marshal.

Proctor   Elizabeth, tell the truth!

Danforth   She has spoken. Remove her!

Proctor (*crying out*)   Elizabeth, I have confessed it!

Elizabeth   Oh, God! (*The door closes behind her.*)

Proctor   She only thought to save my name!

Hale   Excellency, it is a natural lie to tell; I beg you, stop now before another is condemned! I may shut my conscience to it no more – private vengeance is working through this testimony! From the beginning this man has struck me true. By my oath to Heaven, I believe him now, and I pray you call back his wife before we –

Danforth   She spoke nothing of lechery, and this man has lied!

Hale   I believe him! (*Pointing at* **Abigail**.) This girl has always struck me false! She has –

Abigail, *with a weird, wild, chilling cry, screams up to the ceiling.*

Abigail   You will not! Begone! Begone, I say!

Danforth   What is it, child? (*But* **Abigail**, *pointing with fear, is now raising up her frightened eyes, her awed face, toward the ceiling – the girls are doing the same – and now* **Hathorne**, **Hale**, **Putnam**, **Cheever**, **Herrick**, *and* **Danforth** *do the same.*) What's there? (*He lowers his eyes from the ceiling, and now he is frightened, there is real tension in his voice.*) Child! (*She is transfixed with all the girls, she is whimpering open-mouthed, agape at the ceiling.*) Girls! Why do you – ?

Mercy Lewis (*pointing*)   It's on the beam! Behind the rafter!

Danforth (*looking up*)   Where!

Abigail   Why – ? (*She gulps.*) Why do you come, yellow bird?

Proctor   Where's a bird? I see no bird!

Abigail (*to the ceiling*)   My face? My face?

Proctor   Mr Hale –

Danforth   Be quiet!

Proctor (*to* **Hale**)   Do you see a bird?

Danforth   Be quiet!!

Abigail (*to the ceiling, in a genuine conversation with the 'bird', as though trying to talk it out of attacking her*)   But God made my face; you cannot want to tear my face. Envy is a deadly sin, Mary.

Mary Warren (*on her feet with a spring, and horrified, pleading*) Abby!

Abigail (*unperturbed, continuing to the 'bird'*)   Oh, Mary, this is a black art to change your shape. No, I cannot, I cannot stop my mouth; it's God's work I do.

Mary Warren   Abby, I'm *here*!

Proctor (*frantically*)   They're pretending, Mr Danforth!

Abigail (*now she takes a backward step, as though in fear the bird will swoop down momentarily*)   Oh, please, Mary! Don't come down.

Susanna Walcott   Her claws, she's stretching her claws!

Proctor   Lies, lies.

Abigail (*backing further, eyes still fixed above*)   Mary, please don't hurt me!

Mary Warren (*to* **Danforth**)   I'm not hurting her!

Danforth (*to* **Mary Warren**)   Why does she see this vision?

Mary Warren   She sees nothin'!

Abigail (*now staring full front as though hypnotized, and mimicking the exact tone of* **Mary Warren**'s *cry*)   She sees nothin'!

Mary Warren (*pleading*)   Abby, you mustn't!

Abigail *and all the* **Girls** (*transfixed*)   Abby, you mustn't!

Mary Warren (*to all the* **Girls**)   I'm here, I'm here!

Girls   I'm here, I'm here!

Danforth (*horrified*)   Mary Warren! Draw back your spirit out of them!

Mary Warren   Mr Danforth!

Girls (*cutting her off*)   Mr Danforth!

Danforth   Have you compacted with the Devil? Have you?

Mary Warren   Never, never!

Girls   Never, never!

Danforth (*growing hysterical*)   Why can they only repeat you?

Proctor   Give me a whip – I'll stop it!

Mary Warren   They're sporting. They – !

Girls   They're sporting!

Mary Warren (*turning on them all hysterically and stamping her feet*) Abby, stop it!

Girls (*stamping their feet*)   Abby, stop it!

Mary Warren   Stop it!

Girls   Stop it!

Mary Warren (*screaming it out at the top of her lungs, and raising her fists*)   Stop it!!

Girls (*raising their fists*)   Stop it!!

Mary Warren, *utterly confounded, and becoming overwhelmed by* **Abigail***'s and the* **Girls***' utter conviction, starts to whimper, hands half raised, powerless, and all the* **Girls** *begin whimpering exactly as she does.*

Danforth   A little while ago you were afflicted. Now it seems you afflict others; where did you find this power?

Mary Warren (*staring at* **Abigail**)   I – have no power.

Girls   I have no power.

Proctor   They're gulling you, Mister!

Danforth   Why did you turn about this past two weeks? You have seen the Devil, have you not?

Hale (*indicating* **Abigail** *and the girls*)   You cannot believe them!

Mary Warren   I –

Proctor (*sensing her weakening*)   Mary, God damns liars!

Danforth (*pounding it into her*)   You have seen the Devil, you have made compact with Lucifer, have you not?

Proctor   God damns liars, Mary!

Mary *utters something unintelligible, staring at* **Abigail**, *who keeps watching the 'bird' above.*

Danforth   I cannot hear you. What do you say? (**Mary** *utters again unintelligibly.*) You will confess yourself or you will hang! (*He turns her roughly to face him.*) Do you know who I am? I say you will hang if you do not open with me!

Proctor   Mary, remember the angel Raphael – do that which is good and –

Abigail (*pointing upward*)   The wings! Her wings are spreading! Mary, please, don't, don't – !

Hale   I see nothing, Your Honor!

Danforth   Do you confess this power! (*He is an inch from her face.*) Speak!

Abigail   She's going to come down! She's walking the beam!

Danforth   Will you speak!

Mary Warren (*staring in horror*)   I cannot!

Girls   I cannot!

Parris   Cast the Devil out! Look him in the face! Trample him! We'll save you, Mary, only stand fast against him and –

Abigail (*looking up*)   Look out! She's coming down!

She and all the **Girls** *run to one wall, shielding their eyes. And now, as though cornered, they let out a gigantic scream, and* **Mary**, *as though infected, opens her mouth and screams with them. Gradually* **Abigail** *and the* **Girls** *leave off, until only* **Mary** *is left there, staring up at the 'bird', screaming madly. All watch her, horrified by this evident fit.* **Proctor** *strides to her.*

Proctor   Mary, tell the Governor what they – (*He has hardly got a word out, when, seeing him coming for her, she rushes out of his reach, screaming in horror.*)

Mary Warren   Don't touch me – don't touch me! (*At which the* **Girls** *halt at the door.*)

Proctor (*astonished*)   Mary!

Mary Warren (*pointing at* **Proctor**)   You're the Devil's man!

He is stopped in his tracks.

Parris   Praise God!

Girls   Praise God!

Proctor (*numbed*)   Mary, how – ?

Mary Warren   I'll not hang with you! I love God, I love God.

Danforth (*to* **Mary**)   He bid you do the Devil's work?

Mary Warren (*hysterically, indicating* **Proctor**)   He come at me by night and every day to sign, to sign, to –

Danforth   Sign what?

Parris   The Devil's book? He come with a book?

Mary Warren (*hysterically, pointing at* **Proctor**, *fearful of him*) My name, he want my name. 'I'll murder you,' he says, 'if my wife hangs! We must go and overthrow the court,' he says!

Danforth's *head jerks toward* **Proctor**, *shock and horror in his face.*

Proctor (*turning, appealing to* **Hale**)   Mr Hale!

Mary Warren (*her sobs beginning*)   He wake me every night, his eyes were like coals and his fingers claw my neck, and I sign, I sign . . .

Hale   Excellency, this child's gone wild!

Proctor (*as* **Danforth**'s *wide eyes pour on him*)   Mary, Mary!

Mary Warren (*screaming at him*)   No, I love God; I go your way no more. I love God, I bless God. (*Sobbing, she rushes to* **Abigail**.) Abby, Abby, I'll never hurt you more! (*They all watch, as* **Abigail**, *out of her infinite charity, reaches out and draws the sobbing* **Mary** *to her, and then looks up to* **Danforth**.)

Danforth (*to* **Proctor**)   What are you? (**Proctor** *is beyond speech in his anger.*) You are combined with anti-Christ, are you not? I have seen your power; you will not deny it! What say you, Mister?

Hale   Excellency –

Danforth   I will have nothing from you, Mr Hale! (*To* **Proctor**.) Will you confess yourself befouled with Hell, or do you keep that black allegiance yet? What say you?

Proctor (*his mind wild, breathless*)   I say – I say – God is dead!

Parris   Hear it, hear it!

Proctor (*laughs insanely, then*)   A fire, a fire is burning! I hear the boot of Lucifer, I see his filthy face! And it is my face, and yours, Danforth! For them that quail to bring men out of ignorance, as I have quailed, and as you quail now when you know in all your black hearts that this be fraud – God damns our kind especially, and we will burn, we will burn together!

Danforth   Marshal! Take him and Corey with him to the jail!

Hale (*starting across to the door*)   I denounce these proceedings!

Proctor   You are pulling Heaven down and raising up a whore!

Hale   I denounce these proceedings, I quit this court! (*He slams the door to the outside behind him.*)

Danforth (*calling to him in a fury*)   Mr Hale! Mr Hale!

Curtain.

Act Four

A cell in Salem jail, that fall.

At the back is a high barred window; near it, a great, heavy door. Along the walls are two benches.

The place is in darkness but for the moonlight seeping through the bars. It appears empty. Presently footsteps are heard coming down a corridor beyond the wall, keys rattle, and the door swings open. **Marshal Herrick** *enters with a lantern.*

He is nearly drunk, and heavy-footed. He goes to a bench and nudges a bundle of rags lying on it.

Herrick   Sarah, wake up! Sarah Good! (*He then crosses to the other bench.*)

Sarah Good (*rising in her rags*)   Oh, Majesty! Comin', comin'! Tituba, he's here, His Majesty's come!

Herrick   Go to the north cell; this place is wanted now. (*He hangs his lantern on the wall.* **Tituba** *sits up.*)

Tituba   That don't look to me like His Majesty; look to me like the marshal.

Herrick (*taking out a flask*)   Get along with you now, clear this place. (*He drinks, and* **Sarah Good** *comes and peers up into his face.*)

Sarah Good   Oh, is it you, Marshal! I thought sure you be the Devil comin' for us. Could I have a sip of cider for me goin'-away?

Herrick (*handing her the flask*)   And where are you off to, Sarah?

Tituba (*as* **Sarah** *drinks*)   We goin' to Barbados, soon the Devil gits here with the feathers and the wings.

Herrick   Oh? A happy voyage to you.

Sarah Good   A pair of bluebirds wingin' southerly, the two of us! Oh, it be a grand transformation, Marshal! (*She raises the flask to drink again.*)

Herrick (*taking the flask from her lips*)   You'd best give me that or you'll never rise off the ground. Come along now.

Tituba   I'll speak to him for you, if you desires to come along, Marshal.

Herrick   I'd not refuse it, Tituba; it's the proper morning to fly into Hell.

Tituba   Oh, it be no Hell in Barbados. Devil, him be pleasure-man in Barbados, him be singin' and dancin' in Barbados. It's you folks – you riles him up 'round here; it be too cold 'round here for that Old Boy. He freeze his soul in Massachusetts, but in Barbados he just as sweet and – (*A bellowing cow is heard, and* **Tituba** *leaps up and calls to the window.*) Aye, sir! That's him, Sarah!

Sarah Good   I'm here, Majesty! (*They hurriedly pick up their rags as* **Hopkins**, *a guard, enters.*)

Hopkins   The Deputy Governor's arrived.

Herrick (*grabbing* **Tituba**)   Come along, come along.

Tituba (*resisting him*)   No, he comin' for me. I goin' home!

Herrick (*pulling her to the door*)   That's not Satan, just a poor old cow with a hatful of milk. Come along now, out with you!

Tituba (*calling to the window*)   Take me home, Devil! Take me home!

Sarah Good (*following the shouting* **Tituba** *out*)   Tell him I'm goin', Tituba! Now you tell him Sarah Good is goin' too!

In the corridor outside **Tituba** *calls out, 'Take me home, Devil; Devil take me home!' and* **Hopkins***'s voice orders her to move on.* **Herrick** *returns and begins to push old rags and straw into a corner. Hearing footsteps, he turns, and enter* **Danforth** *and* **Judge Hathorne**. *They are in greatcoats and wear hats against the bitter cold. They are followed in by* **Cheever**, *who carries a dispatch case and a flat wooden box containing his writing materials.*

Herrick   Good morning, Excellency.

Danforth   Where is Mr Parris?

Herrick   I'll fetch him. (*He starts for the door.*)

Danforth   Marshal. (**Herrick** *stops.*) When did Reverend Hale arrive?

Herrick   It were toward midnight, I think.

Danforth (*suspiciously*)   What is he about here?

Herrick   He goes among them that will hang, sir. And he prays with them. He sits with Goody Nurse now. And Mr Parris with him.

Danforth   Indeed. That man have no authority to enter here, Marshal. Why have you let him in?

Herrick   Why, Mr Parris command me, sir. I cannot deny him.

Danforth   Are you drunk, Marshal?

Herrick   No, sir; it is a bitter night, and I have no fire here.

Danforth (*containing his anger*)   Fetch Mr Parris.

Herrick   Aye, sir.

Danforth   There is a prodigious stench in this place.

Herrick   I have only now cleared the people out for you.

Danforth   Beware hard drink, Marshal.

Herrick   Aye, sir. (*He waits an instant for further orders. But* **Danforth***, in dissatisfaction, turns his back on him, and* **Herrick** *goes out. There is a pause.* **Danforth** *stands in thought.*)

Hathorne   Let you question Hale, Excellency; I should not be surprised he have been preaching in Andover lately.

Danforth   We'll come to that; speak nothing of Andover. Parris prays with him. That's strange. (*He blows on his hands, moves toward the window, and looks out.*)

Hathorne   Excellency, I wonder if it be wise to let Mr Parris so continuously with the prisoners. (**Danforth** *turns to him,* *interested.*) I think, sometimes, the man has a mad look these days.

Danforth   Mad?

Hathorne   I met him yesterday coming out of his house, and I bid him good morning – and he wept and went his way. I think it is not well the village sees him so unsteady.

Danforth   Perhaps he have some sorrow.

Cheever (*stamping his feet against the cold*)   I think it be the cows, sir.

Danforth   Cows?

Cheever   There be so many cows wanderin' the highroads, now their masters are in the jails, and much disagreement who they will belong to now. I know Mr Parris be arguin' with farmers all yesterday – there is great contention, sir, about the cows. Contention make him weep, sir; it were always a man that weep for contention. (*He turns, as do* **Hathorne** *and* **Danforth**, *hearing someone coming up the corridor.* **Danforth** *raises his head as* **Parris** *enters. He is gaunt, frightened, and sweating in his greatcoat.*)

Parris (*to* **Danforth**, *instantly*)   Oh, good morning, sir, thank you for coming, I beg your pardon wakin' you so early. Good morning, Judge Hathorne.

Danforth   Reverend Hale have no right to enter this –

Parris   Excellency, a moment. (*He hurries back and shuts the door.*)

Hathorne   Do you leave him alone with the prisoners?

Danforth   What's his business here?

Parris (*prayerfully holding up his hands*)   Excellency, hear me. It is a providence. Reverend Hale has returned to bring Rebecca Nurse to God.

Danforth (*surprised*)   He bids her confess?

Parris (*sitting*)   Hear me. Rebecca have not given me a word this three month since she came. Now she sits with him, and her sister and Martha Corey and two or three others, and he pleads with them, confess their crimes and save their lives.

Danforth   Why – this is indeed a providence. And they soften, they soften?

Parris   Not yet, not yet. But I thought to summon you, sir, that we might think on whether it be not wise, to – (*He dares not say it.*) I had thought to put a question, sir, and I hope you will not –

Danforth   Mr Parris, be plain, what troubles you?

Parris   There is news, sir, that the court – the court must reckon with. My niece, sir, my niece – I believe she has vanished.

Danforth   Vanished!

Parris   I had thought to advise you of it earlier in the week, but –

Danforth   Why? How long is she gone?

Parris   This be the third night. You see, sir, she told me she would stay a night with Mercy Lewis. And next day, when she does not return, I send to Mr Lewis to inquire. Mercy told him she would sleep in *my* house for a night.

Danforth   They are both gone?!

Parris (*in fear of him*)   They are, sir.

Danforth (*alarmed*)   I will send a party for them. Where may they be?

Parris   Excellency, I think they be aboard a ship. (**Danforth** *stands agape.*) My daughter tells me how she heard them speaking of ships last week, and tonight I discover my – my strongbox is broke into. (*He presses his fingers against his eyes to keep back tears.*)

Hathorne (*astonished*)   She have robbed you?

Parris   Thirty-one pound is gone. I am penniless. (*He covers his face and sobs.*)

Danforth   Mr Parris, you are a brainless man! (*He walks in thought, deeply worried.*)

Parris   Excellency, it profit nothing you should blame me.
I cannot think they would run off except they fear to keep in
Salem any more. (*He is pleading.*) Mark it, sir, Abigail had close
knowledge of the town, and since the news of Andover has
broken here –

Danforth   Andover is remedied. The court returns there on
Friday, and will resume examinations.

Parris   I am sure of it, sir. But the rumor here speaks
rebellion in Andover, and it –

Danforth   There is no rebellion in Andover!

Parris   I tell you what is said here, sir. Andover have thrown
out the court, they say, and will have no part of witchcraft.
There be a faction here, feeding on that news, and I tell you
true, sir, I fear there will be riot here.

Hathorne   Riot! Why at every execution I have seen naught
but high satisfaction in the town.

Parris   Judge Hathorne – it were another sort that hanged
till now. Rebecca Nurse is no Bridget that lived three year with
Bishop before she married him. John Proctor is not Isaac Ward
that drank his family to ruin. (*To* **Danforth**.) I would to God
it were not so, Excellency, but these people have great weight
yet in the town. Let Rebecca stand upon the gibbet and send
up some righteous prayer, and I fear she'll wake a vengeance
on you.

Hathorne   Excellency, she is condemned a witch. The court
have –

Danforth (*in deep concern, raising a hand to* **Hathorne**)   Pray
you. (*To* **Parris**.) How do you propose, then?

Parris   Excellency, I would postpone these hangin's for a
time.

Danforth   There will be no postponement.

Parris   Now Mr Hale's returned, there is hope, I think – for
if he bring even one of these to God, that confession surely

damns the others in the public eye, and none may doubt more
that they are all linked to Hell. This way, unconfessed and
claiming innocence, doubts are multiplied, many honest people
will weep for them, and our good purpose is lost in their tears.

Danforth (*after thinking a moment, then going to* **Cheever**)   Give
me the list.

Cheever *opens the dispatch case, searches.*

Parris   It cannot be forgot, sir, that when I summoned the
congregation for John Proctor's excommunication there were
hardly thirty people come to hear it. That speak a discontent,
I think, and –

Danforth (*studying the list*)   There will be no postponement.

Parris   Excellency –

Danforth   Now, sir – which of these in your opinion may be
brought to God? I will myself strive with him till dawn. (*He hands
the list to* **Parris**, *who merely glances at it.*)

Parris   There is not sufficient time till dawn.

Danforth   I shall do my utmost. Which of them do you
have hope for?

Parris (*not even glancing at the list now, and in a quavering voice,
quietly*)   Excellency – a dagger – (*He chokes up.*)

Danforth   What do you say?

Parris   Tonight, when I open my door to leave my house –
a dagger clattered to the ground. (*Silence.* **Danforth** *absorbs this.
Now* **Parris** *cries out.*) You cannot hang this sort. There is danger
for me. I dare not step outside at night!

Reverend Hale *enters. They look at him for an instant in silence. He
is steeped in sorrow, exhausted, and more direct than he ever was.*

Danforth   Accept my congratulations, Reverend Hale; we
are gladdened to see you returned to your good work.

Hale (*coming to* **Danforth** *now*)   You must pardon them. They
will not budge.

Herrick *enters, waits.*

Danforth (*conciliatory*)   You misunderstand, sir; I cannot pardon these when twelve are already hanged for the same crime. It is not just.

Parris (*with failing heart*)   Rebecca will not confess?

Hale   The sun will rise in a few minutes. Excellency, I must have more time.

Danforth   Now hear me, and beguile yourselves no more. I will not receive a single plea for pardon or postponement. Them that will not confess will hang. Twelve are already executed; the names of these seven are given out, and the village expects to see them die this morning. Postponement now speaks a floundering on my part; reprieve or pardon must cast doubt upon the guilt of them that died till now. While I speak God's law, I will not crack its voice with whimpering. If retaliation is your fear, know this – I should hang ten thousand that dared to rise against the law, and an ocean of salt tears could not melt the resolution of the statutes. Now draw yourselves up like men and help me, as you are bound by Heaven to do. Have you spoken with them all, Mr Hale?

Hale   All but Proctor. He is in the dungeon.

Danforth (*to* **Herrick**)   What's Proctor's way now?

Herrick   He sits like some great bird; you'd not know he lived except he will take food from time to time.

Danforth (*after thinking a moment*)   His wife – his wife must be well on with child now.

Herrick   She is, sir.

Danforth   What think you, Mr Parris? You have closer knowledge of this man; might her presence soften him?

Parris   It is possible, sir. He have not laid eyes on her these three months. I should summon her.

Danforth (*to* **Herrick**)   Is he yet adamant? Has he struck at you again?

Herrick   He cannot, sir, he is chained to the wall now.

Danforth (*after thinking on it*)   Fetch Goody Proctor to me. Then let you bring him up.

Herrick   Aye, sir. (**Herrick** *goes. There is silence.*)

Hale   Excellency, if you postpone a week and publish to the town that you are striving for their confessions, that speak mercy on your part, not faltering.

Danforth   Mr Hale, as God have not empowered me like Joshua to stop this sun from rising, so I cannot withhold from them the perfection of their punishment.

Hale (*harder now*)   If you think God wills you to raise rebellion, Mr Danforth, you are mistaken!

Danforth (*instantly*)   You have heard rebellion spoken in the town?

Hale   Excellency, there are orphans wandering from house to house; abandoned cattle bellow on the highroads, the stink of rotting crops hangs everywhere, and no man knows when the harlots' cry will end his life – and you wonder yet if rebellion's spoke? Better you should marvel how they do not burn your province!

Danforth   Mr Hale, have you preached in Andover this month?

Hale   Thank God they have no need of me in Andover.

Danforth   You baffle me, sir. Why have you returned here?

Hale   Why, it is all simple. I come to do the Devil's work. I come to counsel Christians they should belie themselves. (*His sarcasm collapses.*) There is blood on my head! Can you not see the blood on my head!!

Parris   Hush! (*For he has heard footsteps. They all face the door.* **Herrick** *enters with* **Elizabeth***. Her wrists are linked by heavy chain, which* **Herrick** *now removes. Her clothes are dirty; her face is pale and gaunt.* **Herrick** *goes out.*)

Danforth (*very politely*)   Goody Proctor. (*She is silent.*) I hope you are hearty?

Elizabeth (*as a warning reminder*)   I am yet six month before my time.

Danforth   Pray be at your ease, we come not for your life. We – (*Uncertain how to plead, for he is not accustomed to it.*) Mr Hale, will you speak with the woman?

Hale   Goody Proctor, your husband is marked to hang this morning.

Pause.

Elizabeth (*quietly*)   I have heard it.

Hale   You know, do you not, that I have no connection with the court? (*She seems to doubt it.*) I come of my own, Goody Proctor. I would save your husband's life, for if he is taken I count myself his murderer. Do you understand me?

Elizabeth   What do you want of me?

Hale   Goody Proctor, I have gone this three month like our Lord into the wilderness. I have sought a Christian way, for damnation's doubled on a minister who counsels men to lie.

Hathorne   It is no lie, you cannot speak of lies.

Hale   It is a lie! They are innocent!

Danforth   I'll hear no more of that!

Hale (*continuing to* **Elizabeth**)   Let you not mistake your duty as I mistook my own. I came into this village like a bridegroom to his beloved, bearing gifts of high religion; the very crowns of holy law I brought, and what I touched with my bright confidence, it died; and where I turned the eye of my great faith, blood flowed up. Beware, Goody Proctor – cleave to no faith when faith brings blood. It is mistaken law that leads you to sacrifice. Life, woman, life is God's most precious gift; no principle, however glorious, may justify the taking of it. I beg you, woman, prevail upon your husband to confess. Let him give his lie. Quail not before God's judgment in this, for it may well be God damns a liar less than he that throws his life away for pride. Will you plead with him? I cannot think he will listen to another.

Elizabeth (*quietly*)   I think that be the Devil's argument.

Hale (*with a climactic desperation*)   Woman, before the laws of God we are as swine! We cannot read His will!

Elizabeth   I cannot dispute with you, sir; I lack learning for it.

Danforth (*going to her*)   Goody Proctor, you are not summoned here for disputation. Be there no wifely tenderness within you? He will die with the sunrise. Your husband. Do you understand it? (*She only looks at him.*) What say you? Will you contend with him? (*She is silent.*) Are you stone? I tell you true, woman, had I no other proof of your unnatural life, your dry eyes now would be sufficient evidence that you delivered up your soul to Hell! A very ape would weep at such calamity! Have the devil dried up any tear of pity in you? (*She is silent.*) Take her out. It profit nothing she should speak to him!

Elizabeth (*quietly*)   Let me speak with him, Excellency.

Parris (*with hope*)   You'll strive with him? (*She hesitates.*)

Danforth   Will you plead for his confession or will you not?

Elizabeth   I promise nothing. Let me speak with him.

A sound – the sibilance of dragging feet on stone. They turn. A pause. **Herrick** *enters with* **John Proctor**. *His wrists are chained. He is another man, bearded, filthy, his eyes misty as though webs had overgrown them. He halts inside the doorway, his eye caught by the sight of* **Elizabeth**. *The emotion flowing between them prevents anyone from speaking for an instant. Now* **Hale**, *visibly affected, goes to* **Danforth** *and speaks quietly.*

Hale   Pray, leave them, Excellency.

Danforth (*pressing* **Hale** *impatiently aside*)   Mr Proctor, you have been notified, have you not? (**Proctor** *is silent, staring at* **Elizabeth**.) I see light in the sky, Mister; let you counsel with

your wife, and may God help you turn your back on Hell.
(**Proctor** *is silent, staring at* **Elizabeth**.)

Hale (*quietly*)   Excellency, let –

Danforth *brushes past* **Hale** *and walks out.* **Hale** *follows.*

Cheever *stands and follows,* **Hathorne** *behind.* **Herrick** *goes.*
Parris, *from a safe distance, offers:*

Parris   If you desire a cup of cider, Mr Proctor, I am sure I –
(**Proctor** *turns an icy stare at him, and he breaks off.* **Parris** *raises
his palms toward* **Proctor**.) God lead you now. (**Parris** *goes out.*)

Alone, **Proctor** *walks to her, halts. It is as though they stood in a
spinning world. It is beyond sorrow, above it. He reaches out his hand as
though toward an embodiment not quite real, and as he touches her, a
strange soft sound, half laughter, half amazement, comes from his throat.
He pats her hand. She covers his hand with hers. And then, weak, he sits.
Then she sits, facing him.*

Proctor   The child?

Elizabeth   It grows.

Proctor   There is no word of the boys?

Elizabeth   They're well. Rebecca's Samuel keeps them.

Proctor   You have not seen them?

Elizabeth   I have not. (*She catches a weakening in herself and
downs it.*)

Proctor   You are a – marvel, Elizabeth.

Elizabeth   You – have been tortured?

Proctor   Aye. (*Pause. She will not let herself be drowned in the sea
that threatens her.*) They come for my life now.

Elizabeth   I know it.

Pause.

Proctor   None – have yet confessed?

Elizabeth   There be many confessed.

Proctor   Who are they?

Elizabeth   There be a hundred or more, they say. Goody Ballard is one; Isaiah Goodkind is one. There be many.

Proctor   Rebecca?

Elizabeth   Not Rebecca. She is one foot in Heaven now; naught may hurt her more.

Proctor   And Giles?

Elizabeth   You have not heard of it?

Proctor   I hear nothin', where I am kept.

Elizabeth   Giles is dead.

He looks at her incredulously.

Proctor   When were he hanged?

Elizabeth (*quietly, factually*)   He were not hanged. He would not answer aye or nay to his indictment; for if he denied the charge they'd hang him surely, and auction out his property. So he stand mute, and died Christian under the law. And so his sons will have his farm. It is the law, for he could not be condemned a wizard without he answer the indictment, aye or nay.

Proctor   Then how does he die?

Elizabeth (*gently*)   They press him, John.

Proctor   Press?

Elizabeth   Great stones they lay upon his chest until he plead aye or nay. (*With a tender smile for the old man.*) They say he give them but two words. 'More weight,' he says. And died.

Proctor (*numbed – a thread to weave into his agony*)   'More weight.'

Elizabeth   Aye. It were a fearsome man, Giles Corey.

Pause.

Proctor (*with great force of will, but not quite looking at her*)   I have been thinking I would confess to them, Elizabeth. (*She shows nothing.*) What say you? If I give them that?

Elizabeth   I cannot judge you, John.

Pause.

Proctor (*simply – a pure question*)   What would you have me do?

Elizabeth   As you will, I would have it. (*Slight pause.*) I want you living, John. That's sure.

Proctor (*pauses, then with a flailing of hope*)   Giles's wife? Have she confessed?

Elizabeth   She will not.

Pause.

Proctor   It is a pretense, Elizabeth.

Elizabeth   What is?

Proctor   I cannot mount the gibbet like a saint. It is a fraud. I am not that man. (*She is silent.*) My honesty is broke, Elizabeth; I am no good man. Nothing's spoiled by giving them this lie that were not rotten long before.

Elizabeth   And yet you've not confessed till now. That speak goodness in you.

Proctor   Spite only keeps me silent. It is hard to give a lie to dogs. (*Pause, for the first time he turns directly to her.*) I would have your forgiveness, Elizabeth.

Elizabeth   It is not for me to give, John, I am –

Proctor   I'd have you see some honesty in it. Let them that never lied die now to keep their souls. It is pretense for me, a vanity that will not blind God nor keep my children out of the wind. (*Pause.*) What say you?

Elizabeth (*upon a heaving sob that always threatens*)   John, it come to naught that I should forgive you, if you'll not forgive yourself. (*Now he turns away a little, in great agony.*) It is not my soul, John, it is yours. (*He stands, as though in physical pain, slowly rising to his feet with a great immortal longing to find his answer. It is difficult to say, and she is on the verge of tears.*) Only be sure of this, for I know it now: Whatever you will do, it is a good man does it. (*He turns his doubting, searching gaze upon her.*) I have read my heart this three month, John. (*Pause.*) I have sins of my own to count. It needs a cold wife to prompt lechery.

Proctor (*in great pain*)   Enough, enough –

Elizabeth (*now pouring out her heart*)   Better you should know me!

Proctor   I will not hear it! I know you!

Elizabeth   You take my sins upon you, John –

Proctor (*in agony*)   No, I take my own, my own!

Elizabeth   John, I counted myself so plain, so poorly made, no honest love could come to me! Suspicion kissed you when I did; I never knew how I should say my love. It were a cold house I kept! (*In fright, she swerves, as* **Hathorne** *enters.*)

Hathorne   What say you, Proctor? The sun is soon up.

Proctor, *his chest heaving, stares, turns to* **Elizabeth**. *She comes to him as though to plead, her voice quaking.*

Elizabeth   Do what you will. But let none be your judge. There be no higher judge under Heaven than Proctor is! Forgive me, forgive me, John – I never knew such goodness in the world! (*She covers her face, weeping.*)

Proctor *turns from her to* **Hathorne**; *he is off the earth, his voice hollow.*

Proctor   I want my life.

Hathorne (*electrified, surprised*)   You'll confess yourself?

Proctor   I will have my life.

Hathorne (*with a mystical tone*)   God be praised! It is a providence! (*He rushes out the door, and his voice is heard calling down the corridor.*) He will confess! Proctor will confess!

Proctor (*with a cry, as he strides to the door*)   Why do you cry it? (*In great pain he turns back to her.*) It is evil, is it not? It is evil.

Elizabeth (*in terror, weeping*)   I cannot judge you, John, I cannot!

Proctor   Then who will judge me? (*Suddenly clasping his hands.*) God in Heaven, what is John Proctor, what is John Proctor? (*He moves as an animal, and a fury is riding in him, a tantalized search.*) I think it is honest, I think so; I am no saint. (*As though she had denied this he calls angrily at her.*) Let Rebecca go like a saint; for me it is fraud!

Voices are heard in the hall, speaking together in suppressed excitement.

Elizabeth   I am not your judge, I cannot be. (*As though giving him release.*) Do as you will, do as you will!

Proctor   Would you give them such a lie? Say it. Would you ever give them this? (*She cannot answer.*) You would not; if tongs of fire were singeing you you would not! It is evil. Good, then it is evil, and I do it!

Hathorne *enters with* **Danforth**, *and, with them,* **Cheever**, **Parris**, *and* **Hale**. *It is a businesslike, rapid entrance, as though the ice had been broken.*

Danforth (*with great relief and gratitude*)   Praise to God, man, praise to God; you shall be blessed in Heaven for this. (**Cheever** *has hurried to the bench with pen, ink, and paper.* **Proctor** *watches him.*) Now then, let us have it. Are you ready, Mr Cheever?

Proctor (*with a cold, cold horror at their efficiency*)   Why must it be written?

Danforth   Why, for the good instruction of the village, Mister; this we shall post upon the church door! (*To* **Parris**, *urgently.*) Where is the marshal?

Parris (*runs to the door and calls down the corridor*)   Marshal! Hurry!

Danforth   Now, then, Mister, will you speak slowly, and directly to the point, for Mr Cheever's sake. (*He is on record now, and is really dictating to* **Cheever**, *who writes.*) Mr Proctor, have you seen the Devil in your life? (**Proctor**'s *jaws lock.*) Come, man, there is light in the sky; the town waits at the scaffold; I would give out this news. Did you see the Devil?

Proctor   I did.

Parris   Praise God!

Danforth   And when he come to you, what were his demand? (**Proctor** *is silent*. **Danforth** *helps*.) Did he bid you to do his work upon the earth?

Proctor   He did.

Danforth   And you bound yourself to his service? (**Danforth** *turns, as* **Rebecca Nurse** *enters, with* **Herrick** *helping to support her. She is barely able to walk*.) Come in, come in, woman!

Rebecca (*brightening as she sees* **Proctor**)   Ah, John! You are well, then, eh?

Proctor *turns his face to the wall.*

Danforth   Courage, man, courage – let her witness your good example that she may come to God herself. Now hear it, Goody Nurse! Say on, Mr Proctor. Did you bind yourself to the Devil's service?

Rebecca (*astonished*)   Why, John!

Proctor (*through his teeth, his face turned from* **Rebecca**)   I did.

Danforth   Now, woman, you surely see it profit nothin' to keep this conspiracy any further. Will you confess yourself with him?

Rebecca   Oh, John – God send his mercy on you!

Danforth   I say, will you confess yourself, Goody Nurse?

Rebecca   Why, it is a lie, it is a lie; how may I damn myself? I cannot, I cannot.

Danforth   Mr Proctor. When the Devil came to you did you see Rebecca Nurse in his company? (**Proctor** *is silent*.) Come, man, take courage – did you ever see her with the Devil?

Proctor (*almost inaudibly*)   No.

Danforth, *now sensing trouble, glances at* **John** *and goes to the table, and picks up a sheet – the list of condemned.*

Danforth   Did you ever see her sister, Mary Easty, with the Devil?

Proctor   No, I did not.

Danforth (*his eyes narrow on* **Proctor**)   Did you ever see Martha Corey with the Devil?

Proctor   I did not.

Danforth (*realizing, slowly putting the sheet down*)   Did you ever see anyone with the Devil?

Proctor   I did not.

Danforth   Proctor, you mistake me. I am not empowered to trade your life for a lie. You have most certainly seen some person with the Devil. (**Proctor** *is silent.*) Mr Proctor, a score of people have already testified they saw this woman with the Devil.

Proctor   Then it is proved. Why must I say it?

Danforth   Why 'must' you say it! Why, you should rejoice to say it if your soul is truly purged of any love for Hell!

Proctor   They think to go like saints. I like not to spoil their names.

Danforth (*inquiring, incredulous*)   Mr Proctor, do you think they go like saints?

Proctor (*evading*)   This woman never thought she done the Devil's work.

Danforth   Look you, sir. I think you mistake your duty here. It matters nothing what she thought – she is convicted of the unnatural murder of children, and you for sending your spirit out upon Mary Warren. Your soul alone is the issue here, Mister, and you will prove its whiteness or you cannot live in a Christian country. Will you tell me now what persons conspired with you in the Devil's company? (**Proctor** *is silent.*) To your knowledge was Rebecca Nurse ever –

Proctor   I speak my own sins; I cannot judge another. (*Crying out, with hatred.*) I have no tongue for it.

Hale (*quickly to* **Danforth**)   Excellency, it is enough he confess himself. Let him sign it, let him sign it.

Parris (*feverishly*)   It is a great service, sir. It is a weighty name; it will strike the village that Proctor confess. I beg you, let him sign it. The sun is up, Excellency!

Danforth (*considers; then with dissatisfaction*)   Come, then, sign your testimony. (*To* **Cheever**.) Give it to him. (**Cheever** *goes to* **Proctor**, *the confession and a pen in hand.* **Proctor** *does not look at it.*) Come, man, sign it.

Proctor (*after glancing at the confession*)   You have all witnessed it – it is enough.

Danforth   You will not sign it?

Proctor   You have all witnessed it; what more is needed –

Danforth   Do you sport with me? You will sign your name or it is no confession, Mister! (*His breast heaving with agonized breathing,* **Proctor** *now lays the paper down and signs his name.*)

Parris   Praise be to the Lord!

Proctor *has just finished signing when* **Danforth** *reaches for the paper. But* **Proctor** *snatches it up, and now a wild terror is rising in him, and a boundless anger.*

Danforth (*perplexed, but politely extending his hand*)   If you please, sir.

Proctor   No.

Danforth (*as though* **Proctor** *did not understand*)   Mr Proctor, I must have –

Proctor   No, no. I have signed it. You have seen me. It is done! You have no need for this.

Parris   Proctor, the village must have proof that –

Proctor   Damn the village! I confess to God, and God has seen my name on this! It is enough!

Danforth   No, sir, it is –

Proctor   You came to save my soul, did you not? Here! I have confessed myself; it is enough!

Danforth   You have not con –

Proctor   I have confessed myself! Is there no good penitence but it be public? God does not need my name nailed upon the church! God sees my name; God knows how black my sins are! It is enough!

Danforth   Mr Proctor –

Proctor   You will not use me! I am no Sarah Good or Tituba, I am John Proctor! You will not use me! It is no part of salvation that you should use me!

Danforth   I do not wish to –

Proctor   I have three children – how may I teach them to walk like men in the world, and I sold my friends?

Danforth   You have not sold your friends –

Proctor   Beguile me not! I blacken all of them when this is nailed to the church the very day they hang for silence!

Danforth   Mr Proctor, I must have good and legal proof that you –

Proctor   You are the high court, your word is good enough! Tell them I confessed myself; say Proctor broke his knees and wept like a woman; say what you will, but my name cannot –

Danforth (*with suspicion*)   It is the same, is it not? If I report it or you sign to it?

Proctor (*he knows it is insane*)   No, it is not the same! What others say and what I sign to is not the same!

Danforth   Why? Do you mean to deny this confession when you are free?

Proctor   I mean to deny nothing!

Danforth   Then explain to me, Mr Proctor, why you will not let –

Proctor (*with a cry of his whole soul*)   Because it is my name! Because I cannot have another in my life! Because I lie and sign myself to lies! Because I am not worth the dust on the feet of them that hang! How may I live without my name? I have given you my soul; leave me my name!

Danforth (*pointing at the confession in* **Proctor***'s hand*)   Is that document a lie? If it is a lie I will not accept it! What say you? I will not deal in lies, Mister! (**Proctor** *is motionless.*) You will give me your honest confession in my hand, or I cannot keep you from the rope. (**Proctor** *does not reply.*) Which way do you go, Mister?

His breast heaving, his eyes staring, **Proctor** *tears the paper and crumples it, and he is weeping in fury, but erect.*

Danforth   Marshal!

Parris (*hysterically, as though the tearing paper were his life*)   Proctor, Proctor!

Hale   Man, you will hang! You cannot!

Proctor (*his eyes full of tears*)   I can. And there's your first marvel, that I can. You have made your magic now, for now I do think I see some shred of goodness in John Proctor. Not enough to weave a banner with, but white enough to keep it from such dogs. (**Elizabeth**, *in a burst of terror, rushes to him and weeps against his hand.*) Give them no tear! Tears pleasure them! Show honor now, show a stony heart and sink them with it! (*He has lifted her, and kisses her now with great passion.*)

Rebecca   Let you fear nothing! Another judgment waits us all!

Danforth   Hang them high over the town! Who weeps for these, weeps for corruption! (*He sweeps out past them.* **Herrick** *starts to lead* **Rebecca**, *who almost collapses, but* **Proctor** *catches her, and she glances up at him apologetically.*)

Rebecca   I've had no breakfast.

Herrick   Come, man.

Herrick *escorts them out,* **Hathorne** *and* **Cheever** *behind them.* **Elizabeth** *stands staring at the empty doorway.*

Parris (*in deadly fear, to* **Elizabeth**)   Go to him, Goody Proctor! There is yet time!

From outside a drumroll strikes the air. **Parris** *is startled.*

Elizabeth *jerks about toward the window.*

Parris   Go to him! (*He rushes out the door, as though to hold back his fate.*) Proctor! Proctor!

Again, a short burst of drums.

Hale   Woman, plead with him! (*He starts to rush out the door, and then goes back to her.*) Woman! It is pride, it is vanity. (*She avoids his eyes, and moves to the window. He drops to his knees.*) Be his helper! What profit him to bleed? Shall the dust praise him? Shall the worms declare his truth? Go to him, take his shame away!

Elizabeth (*supporting herself against collapse, grips the bars of the window, and with a cry*)   He have his goodness now. God forbid I take it from him!

The final drumroll crashes, then heightens violently. **Hale** *weeps in frantic prayer, and the new sun is pouring in upon her face, and the drums rattle like bones in the morning air.*

Curtain.

Appendix

Act Two, Scene Two

A wood. Night.

Proctor *enters with lantern, glowing behind him, then halts, holding lantern raised.* **Abigail** *appears with a wrap over her nightgown, her hair down. A moment of questioning silence.*

Proctor (*searching*)   I must speak with you, Abigail. (*She does not move, staring at him.*) Will you sit?

Abigail   How do you come?

Proctor   Friendly.

Abigail (*glancing about*)   I don't like the woods at night. Pray you, stand closer. (*He comes closer to her.*) I knew it must be you. When I heard the pebbles on the window, before I opened up my eyes I knew. (*Sits on log.*) I thought you would come a good time sooner.

Proctor   I had thought to come many times.

Abigail   Why didn't you? I am so alone in the world now.

Proctor (*as a fact, not bitterly*)   Are you! I've heard that people ride a hundred mile to see your face these days.

Abigail   Aye, my face. Can you see my face?

Proctor (*holds lantern to her face*)   Then you're troubled?

Abigail   Have you come to mock me?

Proctor (*sets lantern on ground. Sits next to her*)   No, no, but I hear only that you go to the tavern every night, and play shovelboard with the Deputy Governor, and they give you cider.

Abigail   I have once or twice played the shovelboard. But I have no joy in it.

Proctor   This is a surprise, Abby. I'd thought to find you gayer than this. I'm told a troop of boys go step for step with you wherever you walk these days.

Abigail   Aye, they do. But I have only lewd looks from the boys.

Proctor   And you like that not?

Abigail   I cannot bear lewd looks no more, John. My spirit's changed entirely. I ought be given godly looks when I suffer for them as I do.

Proctor   Oh? How do you suffer, Abby?

Abigail (*pulls up dress*)   Why, look at my leg. I'm holes all over from their damned needles and pins. (*Touching her stomach.*) The jab your wife gave me's not healed yet, y'know.

Proctor (*seeing her madness now*)   Oh, it isn't.

Abigail   I think sometimes she pricks it open again while I sleep.

Proctor   Ah?

Abigail   And George Jacobs – (*sliding up her sleeve*) he comes again and again and raps me with his stick – the same spot every night all this week. Look at the lump I have.

Proctor   Abby – George Jacobs is in the jail all this month.

Abigail   Thank God he is, and bless the day he hangs and lets me sleep in peace again! Oh, John, the world's so full of hypocrites! (*Astonished, outraged.*) They pray in jail! I'm told they all pray in jail!

Proctor   They may not pray?

Abigail   And torture me in my bed while sacred words are comin' from their mouths? Oh, it will need God Himself to cleanse this town properly!

Proctor   Abby – you mean to cry out still others?

Abigail   If I live, if I am not murdered, I surely will, until the last hypocrite is dead.

Proctor   Then there is no good?

Abigail   Aye, there is one. *You* are good.

Proctor   Am I! How am I good?

Abigail   Why, you taught me goodness, therefore you are good. It were a fire you walked me through, and all my ignorance was burned away. It were a fire, John, we lay in fire. And from that night no woman dare call me wicked any more but I knew my answer. I used to weep for my sins when the wind lifted up my skirts; and blushed for shame because some old Rebecca called me loose. And then you burned my ignorance away. As bare as some December tree I saw them all – walking like saints to church, running to feed the sick, and hypocrites in their hearts! And God gave me strength to call them liars, and God made men to listen to me, and by God I will scrub the world clean for the love of Him! Oh, John, I will make you such a wife when the world is white again! (*She kisses his hand.*) You will be amazed to see me every day, a light of heaven in your house, a – (*He rises, backs away amazed.*) Why are you cold?

Proctor   My wife goes to trial in the morning, Abigail.

Abigail (*distantly*)   Your wife?

Proctor   Surely you knew of it?

Abigail   I do remember it now. How – how – Is she well?

Proctor   As well as she may be, thirty-six days in that place.

Abigail   You said you came friendly.

Proctor   She will not be condemned, Abby.

Abigail   You brought me from my bed to speak of her?

Proctor   I come to tell you, Abby, what I will do tomorrow in the court. I would not take you by surprise, but give you all good time to think on what to do to save yourself.

Abigail   Save myself!

Proctor   If you do not free my wife tomorrow, I am set and bound to ruin you, Abby.

Abigail (*her voice small – astonished*)   How – ruin me?

Proctor   I have rocky proof in documents that you knew that poppet were none of my wife's; and that you yourself bade Mary Warren stab that needle into it.

Abigail (*a wildness stirs in her, a child is standing here who is unutterably frustrated, denied her wish, but she is still grasping for her wits*)   *I* bade Mary Warren – ?

Proctor   You know what you do, you are not so mad!

Abigail   Oh, hypocrites! Have you won him, too? John, why do you let them send you?

Proctor   I warn you, Abby!

Abigail   They send you! They steal your honesty and –

Proctor   I have found my honesty!

Abigail   No, this is your wife pleading, your sniveling, envious wife! This is Rebecca's voice, Martha Corey's voice. You were no hypocrite!

Proctor   I will prove you for the fraud you are!

Abigail   And if they ask you why Abigail would ever do so murderous a deed, what will you tell them?

Proctor   I will tell them why.

Abigail   What will you tell? You will confess to fornication? In the court?

Proctor   If you will have it so, so I will tell it! (*She utters a disbelieving laugh.*) I say I will! (*She laughs louder, now with more assurance he will never do it. He shakes her roughly.*) If you can still hear, hear this! Can you hear! (*She is trembling, staring up at him as though he were out of his mind.*) You will tell the court you are blind to spirits; you cannot see them any more, and you will never cry witchery again, or I will make you famous for the whore you are!

Abigail (*grabs him*)   Never in this world! I know you, John – you are this moment singing secret hallelujahs that your wife will hang!

Proctor (*throws her down*)   You mad, you murderous bitch!

Abigail   Oh, how hard it is when pretense falls! But it falls, it falls! (*She wraps herself up as though to go.*) You have done your duty by her. I hope it is your last hypocrisy. I pray you will come again with sweeter news for me. I know you will – now that your duty's done. Good night, John. (*She is backing away, raising her hand in farewell.*) Fear naught. I will save you tomorrow. (*As she turns and goes.*) From yourself I will save you. (*She is gone.* **Proctor** *is left alone, amazed, in terror. Takes up his lantern and slowly exits.*)

ECHOES DOWN THE CORRIDOR

Not long after the fever died, Parris was voted from office, walked out on the highroad, and was never heard of again.

The legend has it that Abigail turned up later as a prostitute in Boston.

Twenty years after the last execution, the government awarded compensation to the victims still living, and to the families of the dead. However, it is evident that some people still were unwilling to admit their total guilt, and also that the factionalism was still alive, for some beneficiaries were actually not victims at all, but informers.

Elizabeth Proctor married again, four years after Proctor's death.

In solemn meeting, the congregation rescinded the excommunications – this is in March 1712. But they did so upon orders of the government. They jury, however, wrote a statement praying forgiveness of all who has suffered.

Certain farms which had belonged to the victims were left to ruin, and for more than a century, no one would buy them or live on them.

To all intents and purposes, the power of theocracy in Massachusetts was broken.

Notes

5   *An Overture*: in the original production Miller called Act
    One 'The Prologue' and did not start numbering the
    acts until the one that features Elizabeth and Proctor at
    home together. Both 'Prologue' and 'Overture' convey
    Miller's intent in this initial act to paint the social
    background against which the events of this play take
    place, as that is integral to what we witness. Just as in a
    musical overture, this act contains all of the refrains we
    will later hear repeated in the play: elements of
    materialism, superstition, selfish behaviour, insecurity
    and frustration that will combine to create the unfolding
    events. Given a different society, these atrocities could
    not have taken place, which is partly Miller's point.

5   *air of clean spareness*: Miller wishes to convey the austerity
    of Puritan culture. These are not necessarily evil people,
    but they are people who have reduced their lives to a
    spartan existence. It is a 'spareness' against which many
    in the township have begun to rebel, including the
    Reverend Parris himself with his desire for gold
    candlesticks and the deeds to his house.

5   *meeting house*: this was a large building at the centre of the
    town that was built collectively and paid for by the
    township. It was used for both religious worship and
    town business.

6   *would not have permitted anyone to read a novel if one were
    handy*: the town of Salem had a very restrictive outlook
    on what was considered proper behaviour. Little in the
    way of entertainment was condoned; reading, music and
    dance were all frowned upon. This is why Martha
    Corey's reading habit is considered to be suspicious and
    why even the idea that the girls had been dancing in the

woods is scandalous, whether or not they were wearing any clothes.

6   *potent cider*: while the Puritans punished drunkenness, they were not against drinking alcohol in moderation, and actually considered alcohol a gift from God.

6   *time of the armed camp had almost passed*: the area at the mouth of the Naumkeag River was first settled in 1626 by a group of fishermen and became known as Salem in 1629. While the threat of an Indian attack had been there from the outset, given that they were settling on Native American lands, Salem had been relatively free from outside aggression, although people who came there from other settlements had been less fortunate. By the 1690s many townships had learned to exist peaceably with their indigenous neighbours. Fighting in Salem was mostly of a financial nature and was internally driven.

7   *parochial*: literally, of a parish, which would be a limited area, and here refers to the narrow-mindedness of those who live in Salem.

7   *been persecuted in England*: Puritanism was a Protestant movement that developed in England during the late 1500s. It called for a stronger commitment to Jesus Christ and greater levels of personal holiness. Objecting to what they felt was the growing decadence of the established Church in England, Puritans campaigned for social and political reform. Under Charles I, who had strong Catholic sympathies, Puritans were heavily persecuted and many fled to the American colonies. Charles's abusive suppression was a major factor leading to the English Civil War of the 1640s.

7   *But Virginia destroyed them*: Jamestown, Virginia, had been settled in 1607, but suffered from disease and starvation in its early years, as well as being victim of an Indian massacre in 1622 that killed 347 colonists. While the colony survived, it was not without great cost.

7   *autocracy*: a form of government in which one person has absolute power, to which everyone else defers. This is why Salem allows Danforth and his judges to make

decisions for them, as they live in a culture in which obedience is encouraged.

7   *dedicated folk that arrived on the Mayflower*: a hundred and one Puritans had boarded *The Mayflower* in 1620 to escape persecution in England and to create their own society in which they would be free to live according to their religious beliefs. The passage took them a difficult sixty-five days, and they spent a month finding a suitable place to settle once they arrived, which they called Plymouth. Half of the colonists died within six months of the landing, and life in Plymouth was far more precarious than it was for the people in Salem more than seventy years later.

8   *a revolution had unseated the royal government and substituted a junta*: provoked by the oppressive rule of Charles I, whose religious and political aspirations were cause for alarm, in 1642 the English Civil War broke out between Parliamentarians (on whose side the Puritans fought) and Royalists (who supported the monarchy). A series of conflicts took place during which Charles I was beheaded; the leader of the Parliamentarian forces, Oliver Cromwell, set up a Protectorate to rule what was now called the Commonwealth of England, but was in effect a military dictatorship. Cromwell died in 1658 and the resultant slide toward anarchy led to the re-establishment of the monarchy in 1660, with Charles II as the king, although with restricted powers.

8   *developed from a paradox*: this paradox, meaning something that appears contradictory but could be true, informs much of Miller's work. Here it is created by the tension between individual freedom and social responsibility. Both seem necessary; yet on the surface they appear to be in opposition. Miller's solution, as he suggests further on in the paragraph, is to find a 'balance ... between order and freedom'.

9   *Lucifer*: the angel who led a rebellion against God and was cast out of Heaven with his supporters, to live in Hell, becoming the Devil.

9   *Negro slave*: the Puritans were not against slavery, seeing it

as mandated by God. They were actively involved in the
slave trade, taking both Africans and Native Americans
they captured to the West Indies, and then bringing the
more experienced and docile slaves to mainland
America for work as servants. Tituba is one such slave
who has been brought by Parris from Barbados, where
he had previously worked.

9   *no longer bear to be barred from the sight of her beloved*: Tituba
appears to care for Betty Parris, a detail that both
highlights the father's insensibility and makes this
character more sympathetic, even after she has been
badgered into confessing herself a witch.

9   *be hearty*: be healthy.

9   *God help me!*: this indicates Parris's self-regard, as he
should be praying for his ailing daughter but he is more
concerned about how these events will affect his
standing in the community.

10 *speak nothing of unnatural causes*: things unnatural are
considered the realm of evil and the Devil, as anything
that comes from God is part of nature and the natural
way. Parris is fearful that his daughter's condition might
be seen as devil's work; his reputation will be tainted by
his family connection.

11 *you have not opened with me*: you have not told me the whole
truth.

11 *There is a faction that is sworn to drive me from my pulpit*: the
paranoia of Parris is depicted throughout the play and
leads him to ally himself with whomever he feels is in
power. Here he reveals a belief that there is a group of
people in the township who are actively plotting to
remove him from his ministry. Less a religious figure
than a political entity, his presence in Salem is as divisive
as it should be healing, given his profession.

12 *I cannot blink what I saw*: I cannot pretend that I did not
see what I saw.

12 *it is entirely white, is it not?*: as in 'free from moral
impurity'. In the kind of judgmental society Salem has
become, one's reputation, or good name, is very
important. Parris suspects that his unmarried niece,

Abigail, may not be a virgin or, at the very least, does not always behave as properly as she should.

13   *Goody Proctor*: the term 'Goody', a contraction of 'goodwife', was used within this society's lower social level, in the same sense as we use Mrs today.

13   *How high did she fly*: determined to find scandal, Ann Putnam is convinced that Betty has flown, as all witches were suspected of being able to do.

14   *It is a providence*: related to the care and guidance of God, Putnam uses the term 'providence' to mean a 'godsend', literally, 'it is fortunate'. Putnam feels that God has alerted them to the presence of witches in time for the town to do something to control their presence.

14   *forked and hoofed*: as in the pitchfork and cloven feet of the Devil.

15   *George Burroughs*: historically, George Burroughs, a former minister of Salem, was accused of witchcraft in the trials and hanged.

16   *I have laid seven babies unbaptized in the earth*: Puritans generally practised infant baptism. This was usually performed the first Sunday after birth, but Ann Putnam's children evidently did not live long enough to have the ceremony performed. It was common for Puritan women to be pregnant up to twenty-five times, especially as large families were strongly encouraged. Many infants would not survive, however.

16   *Tituba knows how to speak to the dead*: while Tituba declares herself to be a God-fearing Christian, given her colour and Barbados background, it is assumed by the townspeople that she must dabble in some kind of witchcraft. The suggestion is that she has knowledge of voodoo, with its charms and powers of conjuring to raise spirits from the dead.

18   *Aye, mum*: 'Yes, madam'.

18   *If she starts for the window*: indicating a fear she might try to fly.

19   *What a grand peeping courage you have*: Mercy is pointing out that while Mary was too frightened to participate, she did not mind watching others perform the rituals.

20   *bring a pointy reckoning*: Abigail is threatening revenge if anyone dares to tell the truth of what the girls were doing in the woods.

20   *I have seen some reddish work done at night*: Abigail is connected to darkness and evil from the start, having experienced the deaths of her parents in an Indian attack. The colour red is used in the play to denote both death and sexual sin, both of which taint Abigail.

21   *calumny*: when someone makes false statements with malicious intent. Proctor is so marked because of his bluntness, which has offended people like Putnam and Parris and made them resentful.

21   *I'll show you a great doin' on your arse one of these days*: Proctor is threatening to beat her; one in a series of physical threats that are considered acceptable against a servant girl.

21   *strangely titillated*: though fearful of Proctor's manly strength, Mercy has a sexual response to his threat of violence. This shows her own secret urges in a restrictive society and her inability to suppress them.

22   *clapped in the stocks*: the stocks were wooden frames used for punishment. They were set up in a public place and held the culprit immobile by the feet or head and arms. Abuse and rubbish was then thrown at him or her.

23   *I may have looked up*: in this admission, Proctor could be confessing feelings for Abigail.

23   *You are no wintry man*: cold and without feeling.

23   *I know you*: Abigail means this in both the biblical sense, in that they have had sexual relations, and that she feels she knows what Proctor is really like as a person.

23   *We never touched Abby*: he is not denying they slept together but asserting that they should both act as if they never did.

24   *took me from my sleep and put knowledge in my heart*: a sleep of innocence from which she has woken up after she has had such an intense sexual experience with Proctor. She feels that the township's rule against sex out of wedlock is wrong and unfairly restrictive.

25   *a prodigious sign*: in the sense of ominous.

26   *a charge that had more truth in it than Mrs Putnam could know*:
      the real iniquities to which Ann Putnam falls prey are
      her jealousy of Rebecca and her desire to make others a
      scapegoat for her losses.
26   *their silly seasons*: unexplainable but natural behaviour of
      children.
27   *My Ruth is bewildered*: in the sense of acting unnaturally
      because she is bewitched, rather than simply confused.
27   *This society will not be a bag to swing around your head*: Proctor
      asserts himself and warns Putnam that he will not allow
      him to manipulate the township for his own benefit.
27   *This will set us to arguin' again in the society, and we thought to
      have peace this year*: Salem has evidently been a highly
      divided society for some time and has a history of
      grievances among its townspeople. It will be these
      grievances that feed the fire of the accusations.
28   *There are wheels within wheels in this village, and fires within
      fires*: these words convey Ann Putnam's belief that there
      are conspiracies in the village. Indeed, there are, but
      they seem to be caused by such people as the Putnams
      rather than created against them.
28   *We vote by name in this society, not by acreage*: Proctor wants to
      live in a democratic community in which everyone has
      equal say, no matter how much property they own.
      There are others in town who think differently.
28   *many that quail to bring their children:* parents are fearful that
      Parris's sermons are too upsetting for their children, with
      his constant emphasis on sin and damnation. Puritan
      ministers could sometimes speak for up to four hours,
      and no one was allowed to leave or fall asleep.
29   *There is either obedience or the church will burn*: for Parris
      religion is not sustained through faith and caring for
      others, but through complete, unquestioning obedience.
30   *What, are we Quakers?*: in contrast to a strict Puritan
      society in which the minister held sway, the Quakers
      were more egalitarian, encouraging their members to
      experience spirituality on an individual level. They
      generally had a greater commitment to tolerance.
32   *beyond our ken*: outside of our knowledge.

33 *the necessity of the Devil may become evident as a weapon*: Miller asserts that the concept of the Devil is a human construct used in order to threaten people into behaving as the Church dictates.

33 *Inquisition*: from the twelfth century, the Catholic Church investigated heresy through the Inquisition, a body of monks and clerics who used torture to extract confessions. Heretics were burned to death at the stake.

33 *Luther*: Martin Luther (1483–1546) was the German theologian who initiated the Protestant Reformation.

33 *Erasmus*: Desiderius Erasmus (1466/9–1538) was a Dutch humanist and theologian. He steered a middle course over Reformation and was criticised by both Protestants and Catholics.

33 *the children of a history which still sucks at the Devil's teats*: Miller understood how modern society used the same technique of demonising anyone who did not agree with those in control in order to negate their influence. At the time he was writing the play this was a reference both to how communists viewed capitalists and how communists were being viewed and treated in the capital-driven United States. Both sides tended to set their political beliefs at a moral level, so to take an opposing stance would be equated to allying oneself with the Devil.

33 *succubi*: the plural for succubus, a female demon believed to have sexual intercourse with men while they were asleep.

34 *while there were no witches then, there are Communists and capitalists now*: Miller asserts that while there were people in Salem who probably called on the powers of the Devil, he never believed the Devil or real witches were involved. His play draws a sharp analogy between witch trials and the HUAC hearings. His disgust at HUAC was over the rationale behind the hearings, which to his mind unfairly demonised and destroyed those who might have been – or were – connected to communism.

34 *klatches*: informal social gatherings.

34 *Dionysiac*: Dionysus, the god of wine in Greek mythology, was noted for his drunken revels.

35 *yeomanry*: the common class who owned and cultivated

their own land. Hale sees himself, with all of his book learning, as superior to the farming community that largely made up Salem.

38   *incubi*: the plural for incubus, a male demon believed to have sexual intercourse with women while they were asleep.

40   *Perhaps some bird invisible to others comes to you*: witches were believed to be served by animal-shaped spirits. Hale suggests an invisible bird, which Abigail uses later in the play to undercut Mary's testimony.

40   *In nomine Domini Sabaoth sui filiique ite ad infernos*: Latin for 'In the name of the Lord Sabaoth and of his son, depart to hell.' Hale calls on God and Christ to exorcise whatever evil spirit is afflicting Betty.

40   *any living thing in the kettle*: any cooking pot would be referred to as a kettle, and Hale's concern is that the girls were making a witches' potion in which living things were commonly placed.

41   *She makes me drink blood*: Abigail is connected to blood throughout the play, indicating her sexuality as well as the danger she represents to others. Betty tells us earlier that Abigail willingly drank blood as part of a charm to get rid of Elizabeth, and we know that her accusation here is calculated to divert attention from her own misdoings onto Tituba. Tituba, who has clearly had a trusting relationship with Abigail, is evidently upset by her betrayal.

42   *I don't truck with no Devil*: to 'truck' means to have dealings with or to be in league with someone, the double negative suggesting her lack of education rather than any affirmation.

44   *Did you ever see Sarah Good with him? Or Osburn?*: the interrogator puts words and ideas into the mouth of the interrogated, suggesting who is truly responsible for what happens. It is not the people who do the naming but those who cause the names to be spoken.

46   *The marshal, I'll call the marshal!*: it is Abigail who calls in the arm of the law to collect the people they name, suggesting how much control she has already acquired.

47 *takes a pinch of salt, and drops it in the pot*: a simple gesture
that illustrates Proctor's dissatisfaction with his wife
through his dissatisfaction with her cooking. He salts the
stew behind her back, and then compliments her on it
being well-seasoned, which also carries an implication of
his ability to dissemble as well as his wish to please her.

48 *It's winter in here yet*: Proctor feels that his wife has been
giving him the cold shoulder long enough for his lapse
with Abigail.

50 *where she walks the crowd will part like the sea for Israel*: a
reference to the biblical exodus, when the Jews fled from
Egypt and Moses parted the sea for them to cross and
make their escape. The image emphasises Abigail's
power, as she takes on a prophet-like status in this
religious community.

51 *You were alone with her?*: more evidence that Proctor does
not tell his wife the full truth, albeit to forestall her
suspicions. Instead, it makes her all the more suspicious.

52 *your justice would freeze beer*: Elizabeth is associated with
images of frigidity throughout the play, and here Proctor
accuses her of judging him too rigidly and destroying all
possibility of pleasure.

53 *my wife not wholly well*: Elizabeth has been unwell for
some time; partly the reason why they employed Abigail
to help in the house. This might also be a reason Proctor
turned to Abigail for sexual gratification.

53 *poppet*: archaic term for a small handmade doll. It was
believed that witches used these to torture victims or
make them sick by sticking pins into them.

53 *not Sarah Good. For Sarah Good confessed*: the irony of the
witchtrials was that those who confessed were allowed to
live on in jail, while those who refused to confess or
denied the charges were found guilty and hanged. With
such logic it is little wonder that it was near impossible to
escape suspicion once named.

54 *Why, I never heard you mention that before*: Elizabeth's comment
is to assure us that what Mary is describing is a complete
fabrication, however much Mary believes it to be true.

55 *commandments*: according to the Hebrew Bible, the Ten

Commandments were a list of moral imperatives given by God to Moses. They later became part of Christian teaching.

56   *But she's safe, thank God, for they'll not hurt the innocent child*: not wishing to kill an innocent child, the court would not hang a woman known to be pregnant, but rather incarcerate her until after the baby was born.

56   *I would have you speak civilly to me, from this out*: Mary asserts authority over her employers here, given the status she has gained from being an official of the court. The comment also allows us to understand how poorly these young girls were usually treated by their employers.

57   *There is a promise made in any bed*: Elizabeth here seems more astute than her husband, recognising that when a man sleeps with a girl it engenders a relationship between them that cannot be easily ignored by either party.

59   *The promise that a stallion gives a mare I gave that girl*: Proctor sees his marital lapse as a bestial act without rational intent. The imagery here suggests his self-disgust as he compares his coupling with Abigail to the action of beasts in the field.

59   *She has an arrow in you yet, John Proctor*: Elizabeth believes that her husband still has feelings for Abigail, the arrow being a reference to that which Cupid fires into lovers' hearts. Given the extent of his guilt and the way he spoke to Abigail earlier in the play, she could be right, but he is clearly determined to fight this attraction and respect his marriage vows.

61   *Twenty-six time in seventeen month*: despite having farms to run, Puritans were expected to attend lengthy church services with the whole family every Sabbath, and so going to church less than twice a month would have been frowned upon by the entire community. The fact that Parris keeps an attendance record speaks of his petty nature and desire for control.

62   *there is a softness in your record*: meaning it is lax or negligent. The word choice also implies that it is preferable in this culture to be hard and rigid.

63   *Adultery, John*: it is significant that the single
      commandment that Proctor cannot recall is the one of
      which he is guilty of having broken.

65   *such a woman that never lied, and cannot*: an example of
      dramatic irony, as it will be Elizabeth's lie to save her
      husband's reputation that leads to his arrest.

65   *bound to Satan*: in service to.

67   *if Rebecca Nurse be tainted*: literally, morally corrupt. The
      accusations against the kindly Rebecca seem to be what
      most cause Hale to doubt what is happening in Salem,
      especially after he has questioned her privately.

67   *an hour before the Devil fell, God thought him beautiful in Heaven*:
      refers to the belief that the Devil was originally one of
      God's favourite angels, but he was cast out of heaven for
      trying to rebel.

71   *Abby sat beside me when I made it*: suggests that Abigail has
      used her knowledge of the poppet to cast suspicion on
      Elizabeth.

72   *as clean as God's fingers*: pure or perfect, in the way that all
      parts of God were considered flawless.

72   *Pontius Pilate*: the Roman governor who could have
      prevented Christ's crucifixion but decided to wash his
      hands of the business and let others make the decision.
      Proctor feels that Hale has authority to intervene, but by
      allowing the courts to pass judgment is giving up
      responsibility.

74   *Think on cause, man, and let you help me discover it*: another
      example of dramatic irony, as Hale unwittingly provokes
      Proctor's guilt over his adultery, thus making him feel the
      more responsible for the accusations taking place.

75   *God's icy wind, will blow!*: the Puritan God was not a kind
      and forgiving one, but a stern figure of justice. Proctor
      feels his own guilt deeply; realising that he cannot hide
      what he has done from God, he knows he will face
      punishment.

76   *the reading of fortunes*: even such apparently innocent
      activities as this were considered by strict Puritans to be
      the pastime of the Devil.

77   *Are you gone daft, Corey?*: the term in its historical context

has a stronger connotation, implying insanity rather than foolishness.

78   *I have broke charity with the woman*: Giles feels that his questions about his wife's reading habits have brought these charges on her, and that he has betrayed her.

78   *in proper affidavit*: Danforth is a stickler for rules and expects Giles to submit what he wants to say in a formal, written statement that has been signed by someone who is authorised to administer oaths.

80   *I accept no depositions*: a deposition was a statement given under oath, but intended to be read aloud in court without the witness having to be present. Danforth's refusal indicates his suspicion that Proctor is trying to undermine his court, but also that he might prefer a live witness whom he can bully into submission if he dislikes what they say.

83   *He plow on Sunday*: Puritans were expected to keep the Sabbath holy and do no work from sundown the evening before through the whole of the Sabbath day. Most of that day would be spent in prayer.

83   *Cain were an upright man, and yet he did kill Abel*: the Book of Genesis relates how the previously devout Cain killed his brother Abel. It is unclear as to his motive, although jealousy is implied, as God had shown favouritism towards Abel.

83   *she is pregnant*: this means that they will not hang Elizabeth until after the baby is born, but also that, despite Proctor's adultery, he and his wife have resumed sexual relations.

84   *These are my friends, their wives are also accused*: despite being offered his wife's life for the time being, Proctor cannot back down. He feels responsibility towards his neighbours because his sin has partly caused these events.

86   *remember what the angel Raphael said to the boy Tobias*: Tobit suffered much for his good deeds and was blinded in an accident. The angel Raphael assists Tobit's son Tobias in finding a cure for his father who has been a godly man and does not deserve to suffer. Proctor uses the angel's

words to bolster Mary's resolve: however much she
might fear doing the right thing, no harm will result.

91   *proof so immaculate*: Hale is asking for a higher standard of
evidence than this court has so far required. He is
beginning to doubt the unsubstantiated claims that have
led him to agree that seventy-two people be hanged.

91   *for a man of such terrible learning you are most bewildered*:
Danforth mocks Hale by pointing out that someone who
has read so much should be less uncertain. He sees
himself, with his unswerving determination, as the
superior judge.

91   *ipso facto*: literally, as the result of a particular fact.

91   *Unless you doubt my probity?*: probity in the sense of
absolute moral correctness. Danforth asks this
rhetorically; he does not expect any dissent on the
matter.

92–3 *you are either lying now, or you were lying in court, and in either case
you have committed perjury and you will go to jail for it*: Danforth's
harsh treatment of Mary indicates his reluctance to believe
her. His words are meant to intimidate her into backing
down rather than to elicit the truth.

93   *a very augur bit will now be turned into your souls*: an augur is
a type of drill, and the image Danforth conjures up is a
violent representation of how forcefully he intends to
question them.

94   *We are here, Your Honour, precisely to discover what no one has
ever seen*: the internal contradiction of Parris's words is an
indication of his intrinsic foolishness.

95   *It is not a child*: Proctor's pronoun use indicates his disdain
for Abigail; he no longer views her as human.

99   *a cold wind, has come*: Abigail's words echo Proctor's
prediction from Act Two, connecting the couple and
suggesting that their mutual sin is instrumental in these
events.

100   *I have known her*: in the biblical sense, had sexual
intercourse with her.

100   *In the proper place – where my beasts are bedded*: again Proctor
describes his past relationship with Abigail in bestial
terms.

101 *I have made a bell of my honor! I have rung the doom of my good name*: Proctor is pointing out that, having made such a public confession, his own reputation is ruined along with that of Abigail. Puritans viewed adultery as a capital offence for both the man and woman as they held marriage to be one of the highest sacraments.

103 *it is a natural lie to tell*: Hale asks them to consider that Elizabeth has lied in order to save her husband's reputation, but Danforth insists they take Proctor at his word that his wife cannot lie, an ironic stance given that he next calls Proctor a liar.

104 *Why do you come, yellow bird?*: while Abigail might have got the idea of seeing a bird from Hale's earlier comments, the choice of yellow as the colour has led some to wonder if Miller intended this as an oblique reference to a 1947 Tennessee Williams short story, entitled 'Yellow Bird'. Alma, the heroine of this tale, is the daughter of a minister and descendant of a woman who had been hanged as a witch during the Salem witch trials. Her ancestor was reputed to have a yellow bird, which attacked her enemies. During a long sermon given by Alma's pompous father, she sees this bird and it inspires her to embrace a life of drinking and sexual pleasure. If the allusion is intentional it is clearly ironic, connecting Abigail to both a witch and a hedonist. In the transcripts of the actual examination of Tituba, she speaks of having seen a little yellow bird as a familiar of the devil.

106 *They're gulling you, Mister*: Proctor recognises this is a trick to discredit Mary and calls it such. The fact that he refers to Danforth as 'Mister', rather than 'Your Honour', is a sign of his bluntness and refusal to see any man as his superior, as well as his disdain for Danforth's authority, especially when it is based on what he views as foolish beliefs.

107 *as though infected*: Hathorne had earlier asked Mary to show him how the girls created their performances; she had been unable to do so, given the lack of atmosphere. Ironically, here we see exactly how each girl's growing

hysteria infects the rest, but the judges seem convinced that this performance is genuine.

107 *You're the Devil's man!*: Mary desperately turns on Proctor to protect herself, as it is he alone who pressures her to go against the other girls. When she bemoans being forced to sign her name, it is Parris who supplies the idea of her having signed the Devil's book rather than the deposition she no doubt means.

108 *I say – I say – God is dead!*: a blasphemy in any circumstance but perhaps an understandable one given Proctor's level of frustration at the way his good intentions have been turned against him, belying the words of Raphael to Tobias. He feels at this point that justice itself must be dead, and equates that to God, whom Puritans viewed as the fount of all justice.

108 *I hear the boot of Lucifer, I see his filthy face! And it is my face, and yours, Danforth!*: Proctor thinks that by hiding his adultery with Abigail he has helped cause these events, but he sees Danforth and the rest as partners in crime as they, too, do not allow the truth to be heard. All, therefore, will be damned together. It is such understanding that makes Proctor a tragic hero in that he takes responsibility for what occurs.

109 *I denounce these proceedings*: this is a turning point for Hale as he has been made to realise the injustice of the trials, and now refuses to have any more to do with them.

110 *He is nearly drunk*: Marshal Herrick entering the jail cell drunk and jangling his keys seems to recall the drunken gatekeeper from another famous play about witches, *Macbeth*. It is also evidence of Herrick's distaste for what he has been reduced to doing to his neighbours.

112 *I should not be surprised he have been preaching in Andover lately*: although Danforth denies the reports, rumours that the people of Andover are in rebellion against the authority of the courts have reached Salem. Associating Hale with Andover indicates Hathorne's suspicion that Hale is working against the court.

114 *we might think on whether it be not wise, to –*: Parris's desire to postpone the hangings results from selfish motives, but

his hesitation to say what he wants indicates his fear of Danforth as well as his uneasiness to name what they are about to do.

114 *my strongbox is broke into*: we might ask, why should a minister be hoarding money? That Parris has been robbed has a sense of justice to it, since it hits him where it hurts most.

115 *it were another sort that hanged till now*: one reason the courts were initially supported was that they generally arrested and hanged undesirables whom the townspeople were thankful to see go: vagrants, loose women and drunkards. Rebecca and Martha had far higher standing in society; their deaths could call into question the court's standing.

115 *gibbet*: the structure on which people were hanged.

117 *Postponement now speaks a floundering on my part; reprieve or pardon must cast doubt upon the guilt of them that died till now*: such an argument highlights Danforth's self-concern. He is not worried about sentencing innocent people to death, but about preserving his reputation and justifying his decisions regarding those already killed.

118 *like Joshua to stop this sun from rising*: see Joshua 1:15 and 10:24. Joshua asked God to stop the sun from rising in order to spread terror among his enemies while fighting them in battle.

118 *There is blood on my head!*: Hale has lost all belief in what the court is doing and sees himself as a murderer.

118 *Her clothes are dirty; her face is pale and gaunt*: the descriptions of both Elizabeth and Proctor after their time in jail are meant to shock, to show how this court has seriously harmed those already in its clutches.

120 *I tell you true, woman, had I no other proof of your unnatural life, your dry eyes now would be sufficient evidence that you delivered up your soul to Hell! A very ape would weep at such calamity!*: Has Elizabeth been numbed by events, or does she not view Proctor's impending death as worthy of tears? Her demeanour at this point, given her situation, is extremely stoic, and suggests an inner strength this court can neither break nor understand.

123 *It is a pretense, Elizabeth*: Proctor recognises that the deaths of Rebecca and Martha are unjustified; death will make them martyrs. The 'pretense' is that he is actually unworthy of dying alongside them, since he views himself as a sinner. He plans to confess as a form of self-punishment, to show Salem that he is an evil man.

124 *It needs a cold wife to prompt lechery*: Elizabeth blames herself for her husband's adultery, reflecting that she held herself back and drove him into the arms of another woman.

124 *I never knew such goodness in the world!*: having asked for forgiveness and to transfer his feelings of guilt on to herself, Elizabeth offers a valuation of her husband designed to bolster him against his impending death. She hopes to give him the strength to do what is right. She will not tell him what to do, but her assertion of his goodness implies that it would be wrong for him to confess.

127 *I am not empowered to trade your life for a lie*: Danforth is not satisfied with Proctor's confession; he needs him to name names, to implicate the others they plan to hang. This is the way in which HUAC also operated, and the aspect of the hearings that Miller found the most despicable.

128 *I speak my own sins; I cannot judge another. . . I have no tongue for it*: Proctor is not confessing to witchcraft but his adultery, and this is a crime of which only he is guilty. When Miller was brought to testify before HUAC three years later, he told the committee: 'I take the responsibility for everything I have ever done, but I cannot take responsibility for another human being.'

130 *I have given you my soul; leave me my name!*: this concern with holding on to one's name is noticeable in Miller's plays of this period. Eddie Carbone, from 1956's *A View from the Bridge*, also tries to defend the integrity of his name. During the Red Scare of the 1950s, people whose names were given to HUAC often lost their careers and their livelihoods. But the idea of a 'name' also seems to evoke for Miller the essence of a person, an essence that must be held on to by any individual who wishes to maintain a sense of his or her own selfhood.

130 *I do think I see some shred of goodness in John Proctor*: Proctor has come to recognise the truth of his wife's recent declaration.

131 *It is pride, it is vanity … what profit him to bleed*: Hale cannot see the nobility of what Proctor is doing and views his self-sacrifice as an act of pride, a stubborn refusal to give the court what they want. He fails to acknowledge the moral implications of Proctor's false confession and the value of what he stands for.

131 *He have his goodness now. God forbid I take it from him!*: Elizabeth fully endorses Proctor's decision.

131 *the new sun is pouring in upon her face*: the lighting reference emphasises the transcendent aspects of Proctor's death against its cold reality.

Appendix

132 *I thought you would come a good time sooner*: Abigail's softness toward Proctor suggests that she truly is in love with him, and sincerely thinks that he loves her too.

132 *I had thought to come many times*: Proctor's meaning here is ambivalent. Is he saying he thought to come to her to ask for help with Elizabeth or as a sometime lover? She clearly takes him to mean the latter (which also may be his intention, in order to flatter her into compliance). As the scene progresses, Proctor, finding himself unable to persuade her with words, again resorts to violence by shaking her roughly, though such violence continues to be ineffective.

132 *I hear only that you go to the tavern every night, and play shovelboard with the Deputy Governor, and they give you cider*: Abigail's position in the township has been greatly elevated. She is now treated as an honorary man, allowed in the tavern to drink and play games.

133 *I'm holes all over*: this suggests that Abigail is psychologically distressed, believing that spirits torture her. Given that we are meant to believe there are no witches in Salem, she must be inflicting these injuries

upon herself. It could be that she is doing this consciously in order to give greater credibility to her claims, but the stage directions imply that this may be part of her madness.

134 *you burned my ignorance away*: the references to burning and fire between Abigail and Proctor suggest that their coupling was aligned to hell. It also relates their affair to the play's title. A crucible is a container in which materials are heated to high temperatures in order to change their basic properties.

134 *hypocrites in their hearts*: Abigail is right to view some of the townspeople as hypocrites, but she casts her net too widely, asserting that even such as Rebecca could be counted among these.

134 *How – ruin me?*: more evidence of Abigail's pride and psychological state, as she seems to believe that despite her adultery she remains nonetheless in an unassailable position of right.

136 *Fear naught. I will save you tomorrow … From yourself I will save you*: Abigail still hopes that she can win Proctor for herself.

Questions for Further Study

1 In what ways can you view John Proctor as a tragic hero?
2 Who do you see as the most evil character in the play, and why?
3 What do you believe causes the girls of Salem to cry out in the way that they do?
4 How far does Tituba's race affect how the people of Salem treat her?
5 In the play, who do you think changes the most and who changes the least?
6 In what ways does *The Crucible* represent morality in conflict with the law?
7 The appeal of the play cannot be attributed only to the Salem witch trials or the Red Scare of the 1950s. Why has *The Crucible* held up so well? What makes it still worth reading and performing?
8 How does *The Crucible* reflect the day-to-day life of seventeenth-century Salem?
9 Analyse the ways in which gender influences the action and relationships presented in *The Crucible*.
10 What is the importance of poetic and stage imagery in *The Crucible*?
11 What insights are gained by the characters of Elizabeth Proctor, Reverend Hale and John Proctor, and what leads them to embrace these new understandings?
12 Assess Miller's claims that *The Crucible* is a companion piece to *Death of a Salesman* in the way that both plays explore the role of the individual in conflict with the dictates of society.
13 To what extent can *The Crucible* be considered an example of stage realism?
14 How far are we meant to accept Elizabeth taking on the blame for her husband's adultery?

15 What does the play suggest about the nature and challenge of marriage?

16 Compare Danforth and Proctor as characters, outlining their motives for action and the way they value and relate to other people.

17 Is sex and sexuality the underlying cause of what happens in Salem?

18 If you were directing a production of *The Crucible*, how would you have the character of Abigail Williams played?

19 In what ways have visual and non-verbal stage effects been used to communicate meaning in the play?

20 To what extent is *The Crucible* a criticism of American society past and present? In what ways is it a critique of other societies?

21 In his hearing before HUAC Miller declared, 'I will protect my sense of myself. I could not use the name of another person and bring trouble on him.' How does this statement parallel John Proctor's stance? What does a 'name' represent to Miller?

22 What are the dangers of interpreting this play in a narrow political sense?

SUSAN C.W. ABBOTSON is Professor of Modern and Contemporary Drama at Rhode Island College and author of *Masterpieces of 20th-Century American Drama, Thematic Guide to Modern Drama, Student Companion to Arthur Miller* and *Critical Companion to Arthur Miller*, as well as *Understanding Death of a Salesman* (co-authored with Brenda Murphy). A specialist on Arthur Miller, she is currently the Performance Editor for the *Arthur Miller Journal*.

ENOCH BRATER is the Kenneth T. Rowe Collegiate Professor of Dramatic Literature at the University of Michigan. He has published widely in the field of modern drama, and is an internationally renowned expert on such figures as Samuel Beckett and Arthur Miller. His recent books include *Arthur Miller: A Playwright's Life and Works, Arthur Miller's America: Theater and Culture in a Time of Change*, and *Arthur Miller's Global Theater: How an American Playwright Is Performed on Stages aound the World*.